FEEDING

THE WORLD
OF
THE FUTURE

Other books by Hal Hellman
in the World of the Future series:

THE CITY IN THE WORLD OF THE FUTURE

TRANSPORTATION IN THE WORLD OF THE FUTURE

COMMUNICATIONS IN THE WORLD OF THE FUTURE

BIOLOGY IN THE WORLD OF THE FUTURE

FEEDING

THE WORLD OF THE FUTURE

BY

HAL HELLMAN

PUBLISHED BY

M. Evans and Company, Inc. NEW YORK

AND DISTRIBUTED IN ASSOCIATION WITH

J. B. Lippincott Company

PHILADELPHIA AND NEW YORK

For the Smolers—and they know why

The author regrets that it is impossible to thank separately the dozens of individuals from various firms and universities who contributed in various ways to this book. Special thanks, however, are due to: Mr. M. O. Whithed, Manager-Agricultural Marketing, Edison Electric Institute, Professor Robert Jones of the University of Missouri, Norman R. Michie, Information Liaison Officer of the Food and Agriculture Organization of the United Nations, Dr. Carl O. Hodge, Research Specialist at the University of Arizona, and Henry Romney, Head of the Information Service at The Rockefeller Foundation, who were particularly helpful in providing information; Mr. D. L. Meldahl, of Archer Daniels Midland Company, who sent samples of that firm's textured vegetable protein (TVP®) for me to try out; and, finally, to Mrs. Marcella Katz, Head Nutritionist at the Health Insurance Plan of Greater New York, and Mrs. Irene Uribe, who has worked closely with The Rockefeller Foundation's agricultural sciences program for several years, both of whom reviewed the manuscript. Their comments and suggestions were very helpful.

Contents

FEEDING

THE WORLD
OF
THE FUTURE

Prologue

ANDREW MANN'S WIFE was away for the holidays, visiting one of her relatives. She had taken Janet along, leaving Andrew and Jeff to fend for themselves for a few days.

Although it was only 11 A.M. Jeff was already hungry. After all, he was normally in school at this time; but today he was helping out with the chores. "How soon can we have lunch, Dad?"

"What? Hungry already? Well, all right. Let's just take a couple of monitor readings and then we'll head back to the house."

They walked across the lawn to the feed lot, and Andrew watched while Jeff pointed the monitor at one of their prize, 14-foot-tall beef cattle.

"Uh uh," said Andrew. "That one doesn't have an electronic monitor in him."

"But I thought you put them in all the steers."

"No. That would be pointless. We just pick out ten or so of them. We can be pretty sure that what's happening in their stomachs is representative of what's going on inside all the others. If these ten are turning the feed mixture into beef at an efficient clip, then we can be pretty darned sure the other four hundred and ninety are too. Here, shoot old 'Redeyes.' He's got one."

Jeff aimed the "staker" (steer data taker) at "Redeyes" and pulled the trigger. Although nothing at all seemed to happen, he knew that a radio service was accepting data from a tiny transmitter in the monitor and taping it. The whole process took no more than 30 seconds for each steer. Later the data would be transmitted by telephone wire to a central computer at the university along with other information about the farm—amount of rations on hand, and so on. The central computer would combine this with its own knowledge about current market prices, weather forecasts, and new information on feed formulas. Any pertinent information would be relayed back to the print-out panel in the house.

"Now can we eat?" asked Jeff.

"Yup," laughed his father.

They hopped into the air cushion runabout and sped across the fields. Jeff was at the controls, and Andrew relaxed. "Sure is nice to have you around, son. It gets real lonely around here since old Jed retired. Sometimes I wonder if I shouldn't just hire someone to keep me company, now that your mother is so busy with her new career."

"You mean Farm Animal Psychology?"

"Um hm."

"How's the music background working out in the milk shed?"

"Well, as you know, that's not really a new idea. It was tried and shown to be useful back in the 1970's. But your mother's experiment are concerned with trying out the newer types of music to see if she can find any way of improving the effect . . . Whoops! Slow down, Jeff. Head on over to that robotrac over there. It seems to have stopped for some reason."

The runabout banked into a smooth turn and came to a gentle stop next to the giant tape-controlled, driverless robot tractor that normally lumbered across the landscape day and night, doing all the various jobs that had to be done.

Andrew walked over to the control panel on the side and asked what was wrong. A printed slip came out saying, "Your instructions were to harvest lettuce. But not a single lettuce head was ready and won't be until tomorrow. I sent an alarm, but it was not answered. So I wait for instructions."

Andrew showed the note to Jeff with a disgusted expression on his face. "Damn that central computer. Can't it get anything right?"

"Hey," exclaimed Jeff, "how come your alarm didn't ring?"

"I was wondering the same thing," said his father, who was searching his pockets. "I guess I forgot to take it with me this morning. Wouldn't you know it? The first time in two years it would have come in handy and I don't have it with me. I wonder how long the robotrac has been out of commission. Oh, well, I can check that as I reprogram. I'm afraid lunch is going to have to wait, Jeff—unless you want to eat alone."

"No. I'll wait. I want to see how you reprogram, anyhow."

The driverless machines on the farm of the year 2000 might be observed on an electronic field map, such as this one, in the farm's control center.

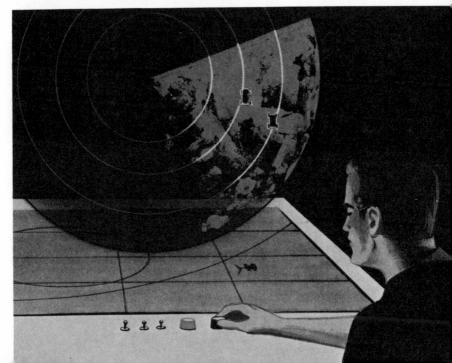

"Well, I can't do that here. Let's get back to the house. I'll have to check some things on the computer first."

"Like what?" asked Jeff as they continued their trip.

"Well, I want to see what the next crop is on the program and whether it's ready for handling. I don't have that with me. I also want to get the computer going on finding out what the problem is with the lettuce. And, finally, we have to get the robotrac going again. I can't afford to let it stand around doing nothing."

At the control console in the house, Andrew began typing on the computer terminal. After he finished inserting the information and questions, there was a moment's pause, and then the typewriter started giving back the needed data.

"Well, I'll be," exclaimed Andrew. "It apologizes . . . Then says it miscalculated the irrigation requirements because of an unexpected change in the weather. And—get this—it says if I had set up all-weather enclosures, as it suggested several years ago, this wouldn't have happened. Son of a gun! What nerve. I've got a mind to tell it to . . ." Suddenly he realized that he was talking about a machine and he and Jeff both burst out laughing. The last time something like this happened, he had called it a "stupid moron,"—in type, of course —and it had answered, "You are right."

"Wise guy. What's next on the program?"

"Carrots. And they're ready to be taken in. But this means I'll have to send the trac back to the maintenance center for a change of gear." He punched out the necessary instructions and flipped on the TV monitor covering that portion of the fields to make sure the robotrac started. It did, and Andrew and Jeff turned their attention to their own stomachs.

Jeff stepped on the scale, set the height indicator, and breathed into the nutrient analyzer. A few seconds later the indicator showed he was slightly low in tryptophan, but noth-

14

ing to worry about. "Hm. I'll have to make that up one of these days," he mumbled.

Andrew had his height and weight already stored in the analyzer, so he only had to identify himself before breathing into it. He was apparently all right in all areas.

"Well, Jeff, what'll it be? We've got some nice fried fillets from Mr. Jackson's catfish farm up the road. They should help you make up the tryptophan. By the way—Mr. Jackson has just leased some acreage on the Continental Shelf. He's branching out into deep water farming."

"Got any whale fillets?"

"No, it's too soon. But we have some great algae pies."

"Good. And some roast beef?"

"The real thing? We've got some fine roasts from our own stock," said Andrew proudly.

All the food on this plate is basically vegetable matter, though it tastes (reading clockwise from lower left) like beef, ham, bacon and chicken.

"Are you kidding? You know I wouldn't touch that stuff with a ten-meter pole. It tastes awful. Don't you have any of the synthetic meat?"

Andrew sighed and punched the proper buttons. Two algae pies and a package of synthetic beef slices made from bean protein and yeast were automatically drawn from storage, cooked in the microwave oven for the proper time —some 30 seconds or so—and then popped out at the proper time.

Andrew figured he'd better change the subject. This was a sore point in the house, with both children much preferring synthetic foods to natural ones. "Well, son, what's doing in school?"

"Oh, I forgot to tell you, I'm transferring out of the agricultural college."

"To where?" Andrew asked.

"To the chemistry department. I decided I want to be a flavorist."

"A what?"

"Don't you know anything? He's the guy who creates all those great flavors in the synthetic foods."

Andrew bit into his synthetic roast beef sandwich, rather harder than was absolutely necessary.

16

1

The Plow vs. the Stork

MOHANDAS K. GANDHI, the spiritual and political leader of India for many years, once said, "If God should appear to an Indian villager it would be in the shape of a loaf of bread."

A spiritual leader saying a thing like that?

In 1943 there was a famine in the region called Bengal. As a direct result, three million people starved to death.

There are an estimated four million persons in India who are completely blind, and perhaps twelve million who are partially blind, mainly because of lack of vitamin A in their diets.

Reasons enough?

Gandhi was referring to the average Indian villager, but he could just as well have been thinking of something on the order of two-thirds of the people in the world. It has been estimated that a third of the world's people live on the edge of starvation, while another third are poorly nourished (not enough of the right food), as well as hungry much of the time.

More than half of all Philippine children under the age of ten are said to be poorly nourished. Nor are the results of this

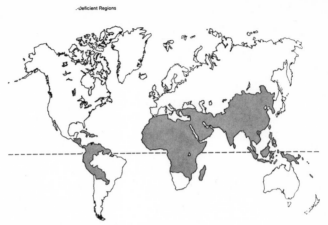

.-Deficient Regions

Two-thirds of the world's people live in food-short regions.

strictly physical. Six or seven per cent of the children under four are probably seriously retarded because of inadequate diet.

Perhaps 10,000 people starve to death somewhere in the world every day—That adds up to 3½ million people a year. Some estimates put this number as high as 20 million per year.

Some 40 million deaths a year are said to be related in some way to hunger. This is two thirds of the total number of deaths. For in addition to starvation, there is the very serious problem of lack of resistance to disease because of poor diet.

After a while the numbers no longer mean anything. Sometimes one needs a personal experience to make things seem real. One American woman I know decided to take a vacation in India. After a few days she became so distressed by the hunger and poverty around her, by the poor children and adults begging, that she simply gave away all the money she had taken with her and returned home.

What's wrong, anyway? How is it that in an age of rockets, color television, and atomic energy man can't produce enough

food to feed everyone? There are two answers. One is that
the people who are producing the rockets are in general not
the ones who are hungry. The world seems, unfortunately,
to be divided into two general classes: the developed countries and the less developed countries. Because we will have
a great deal to say about them, let us use the abbreviations
DC for the first and LDC for the less developed countries.

A DC might be defined as a country in which modern
science has been applied to the agriculture in such a way
that its food production has "taken off." There seems to be
no other way to describe the process. Examples of DCs are
the United States, Canada, Japan, and all of Western Europe.

All attempts by LDCs to skip this process and to jump into
industrialism, with or without help from DCs, have failed.
The country must be able to feed its people first. Then it can
move into industrialism. In most DCs agriculture still provides
more than three-quarters of the exports. Even a country like
Holland, one of the most densely populated in the world, is
self-sufficient in food.

Of course most of the DCs do import food. But this is
largely to provide variety in the diet. (If a poor Asian farmer
is growing rice he eats rice—at every meal—and considers
himself lucky to have something else to put into it.) But the
DCs generally also export other foods. And they could produce
all their food needs if they had to.

This of course does not mean that there are no hungry
people in the DCs. It does mean that *on the average* enough
food is grown or purchased to feed everyone satisfactorily.
There are still millions of hungry people right here in the
United States, for instance, and this is shameful. There are
a million children at or near the poverty level in Britain. And
this too is shameful. But these are economic problems, un-
balances in distribution which have little to do with how
much food is grown or purchased by the country. Indeed one

19

of the major problems with the majority of people in the DCs is that they eat too much!

The second reason presents an even more serious problem. For we are in a race—a race between the plow and the stork, between food production and people production.

Hunger, malnutrition, even starvation are not new problems. The food problem is as old as mankind. What is new is the fact that no matter how fast we increase our production of food (world-wide), our production of people either keeps up or moves ahead. In the last decade the yearly increases in production of food have been as high as 10 per cent. These have been phenomenal increases, unprecedented in the history of man. Yet all we managed to do is about keep pace with the population increase, or move ahead a little bit.

Years ago the numbers of people in the world were held to a fairly steady level by disease, famine, and war. While war, unfortunately, is still a problem, famine and disease have been reduced considerably. As a direct result, the increase in world population in the last 150 years or so has been far, far greater than in the previous 3,000 years. Again, India provides us with a striking example.

According to one calculation, the life expectancy of women in India a quarter of a century ago was 27 years. This meant that the *average* female child could expect to live no longer than 27 years. Now, however, thanks to improved drugs, sanitary conditions, medical care, and, to some extent, better food, the figure has jumped to almost 50 years.

The significance of this lies in more than just the fact that the average woman's life has been extended by almost 100 per cent. She now lives through the entire time of child bearing. Thus we have not one more mouth to feed for another 25 years, but three, five, seven, or even more for 50 years.

The outcome is that the Indian population, which had remained relatively stable at about 100 million for centuries, has

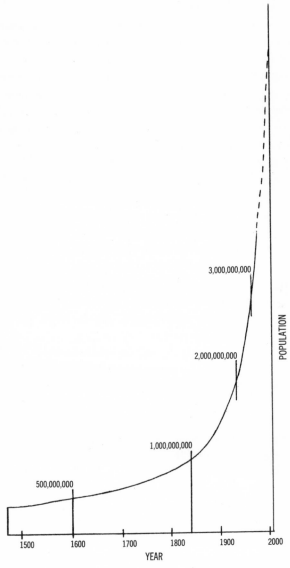

World population is increasing at a fantastic rate.

leaped to over 550 million in the last century and a half and is climbing ever more rapidly.

Nor is this situation peculiar to India. World-wide, the population increase is on the order of 2 per cent a year. This doesn't sound like much. But translated into actual population numbers it means an overall increase of 70 million mouths (at current levels) to feed every year, each of which will consume upwards of 25 tons of food over the course of a lifetime. And by the end of this century 80 per cent of these new mouths will appear in the LDCs, just those countries that can least afford them.

The figure of two per cent is only an average. The LDCs are producing children at double the rate of DCs; the highest rates of growth are occurring in Africa and Latin America. In the latter region the figure is almost three per cent; at this rate of increase the population of a country will multiply by two in twenty-four years (one generation) and by sixteen in a century!

A Strange Situation

How is it that the rates are so much higher in the LDCs? There are a number of reasons, but the main one has to do with a desire for some kind of "social security." The LDC governments are simply too poor to be able to provide any kind of monetary social security, so the people, most of whom are farmers, must find another approach. And this is where the trouble lies.

Four-fifths of the farmers in LDCs live at what is called a subsistence level. This means that the man and his family have only what they grow to eat. If the crops fail they go hungry; there is seldom anything more than a small amount of food left over to sell or trade for something else. There is no way to put anything away for the future. There is only one hope: have a few sons who will perhaps be able to provide for you when you get too old to do so for yourself.

Not one son, mind you, because he couldn't possibly grow enough extra food all by himself to supply your needs. So it must be several sons. But nature does not always send sons. And of the sons who are born, not all can be expected to survive. So it is that a poor farmer and his wife, who can barely feed themselves, will have six, seven, or even more children in the hopes that at least a few males will manage to survive and help to provide for the parents' old age.

The children particularly suffer cruelly because obviously the father needs all his strength to do the farming that is providing the food in the first place. So he must get enough food even though it may mean that the rest of the family will eat less. But the human body grows to 20 per cent of its adult size in the first three years. Where is the young child to obtain the materials for a sound body if not enough of the right food, or any food, is available?

Even worse, the human brain grows to *80 per cent* of its final size in the same period of time. If it is short-changed, mental retardation is the inevitable result. Undernourished children have been found to lack as much as 20 per cent of the normal amount of brain cells for their age, and IQs have ranged as much as 25 per cent below average.

Anemia, goiter, rickets, and a host of other diseases have also been shown to result from poor food or no food at all.

And so it is that vast numbers of farm families are locked into a vicious cycle of ignorance, poverty, disease, hunger, and weakness. Worst of all is the hopelessness of the situation. They are condemned forever to . . .

But wait.

What we have said up to now concerns the past and the present. As anyone who has ever thought about it knows very well, however, predicting the future is a very tricky business. History is full of predictions that have been proved wrong.

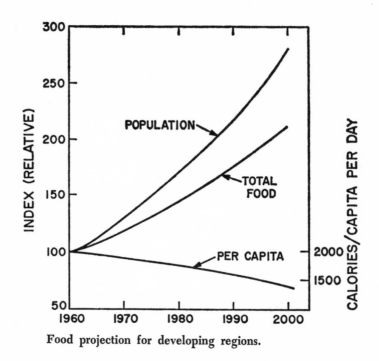

Food projection for developing regions.

Most predictions of the future are based on the past. After all, what other experience do we have to go on? The general approach is to see the future as an extension of the past. But this may or may not be true.

In this book, for example, we are dealing with the quantity and quality of food in the world of the future. Look now at the graph shown here, which was published in 1967. Note that there seems to be, on the basis of what has gone on before, a clear indication of continuing and increasing hunger. In the same year a book was published that predicted world-wide famine by 1975.[*] After all, it was only a year or two

[*] William and Paul Paddock, *Famine—1975!*, Little, Brown & Co., 1967.

earlier that the United States had shipped 40 per cent of its wheat crop abroad as food aid, half of it to India. Over a period of two years 60 million Indians were sustained by these food shipments.

But the experience of the last few years has thrown a new factor into the equation, one that has caused an enormous increase in food production throughout the world—and especially in the LDCs! The point is that the graph is no longer valid, at least not for the present. A new graph would show that, world-wide, food production is increasing fast enough to just about keep pace with the exploding population. What this means is that, although the plow has certainly not yet caught up with the stork, it is no longer losing ground. Whether it can continue to keep pace, or perhaps even catch up, is another question altogether. Perhaps you have heard the story of the young man who did a favor for a king. The king asked him what he would like as a reward. His answer was modest—or so it seemed. He would just like some wheat, and the amount was to be calculated in this way: one grain on the first square of a chessboard; two grains or double that amount on the second square; four grains on the third; eight grains on the fourth; and so on.

The king was extremely pleased until he realized that by the time he would get to the sixty-fourth square, there would not be enough wheat in the entire kingdom to satisfy the number called for. Try the multiplication involved. You'll get tired long before you get to the end. The number turns out to be 2^{64}, a big number indeed.

The story is relevant here because this kind of increase, called *exponential*, is the kind we are seeing in population growth. The basic idea is that each doubling then produces another doubling, and so on.

But food production does not work that way. Its increases are arithmetic, they are not compounded as they are in exponential increases. A doubling of the food production remains just that, a doubling. It does not automatically produce another doubling.*

Also, doubling the amount of water used in irrigation may double your yield; using four times as much may drown all the crops. It is conceivable that the amount of land put into food production can be doubled, but after a very short time there is no place left for cities, roads—or people.

Nevertheless, a major change has taken place during the last few years in the amount and even the kind of food that is being produced. The change is so vast that it has been called a revolution, the "Green Revolution." Not only is it one of the few bloodless revolutions the earth has seen but it is one giving heart to millions of those hopeless farmers we talked about a few pages back.

This does *not* mean—as we saw early in the chapter—that everyone now has enough of the right foods to eat. Some regions, particularly sections of Latin America and Africa, are falling even further behind.

However you look at it, the race between the stork and the plow, between population and food, continues. In broad outline, food production must double as quickly as possible (and distribution must be smoothed out somehow) if we are to eliminate undernourishment and starvation in the world today.

Due to inevitable population increases—barring war, famine, and disease (or preventing them)—food production by the end of the century must quadruple.

---

* Someone is bound to bring up the principle of compounding leverages, so I may as well mention it here. Under this principle, each factor multiplies the effect of whatever happened before. If better irrigation raises the yield by 50 per cent, and improved fertilization also increases the yield 50 per cent, the total increase is not 100 per cent, but 125 per cent. (The second 50 per cent is taken on the new total.) But the increase does not *continue* to compound itself, as in an exponential increase.

The Plow
vs. the Stork

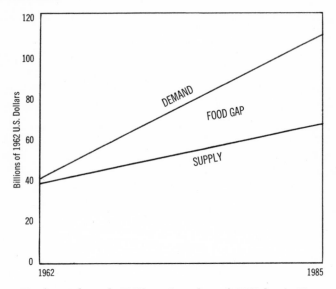

Food gap through 1985, projected as of 1970 by A. H. Boerma, director-general of the Food and Agriculture Organization of the U.N.

Attention is finally being turned to this very important matter; the approaches being taken can be divided, roughly, as follows:

1) Increasing yields
2) Improving the quality of the foods people eat
3) Better utilization of existing food resources (reducing waste, cutting down loss to insects, etc.)
4) Searching out new sources of food

Before we look into these various approaches, it is important that we have a good understanding of the basic food needs of a human being. Many Americans have the idea that the average poor Asian can exist satisfactorily, if not happily, on a bowl of rice a day. This is a cruel delusion. The Asian *is* smaller on the average than the American (probably due in large part to his poor diet). And as a result he may be able to get by on somewhat less food.* But for good health he needs the same mix of proteins, vitamins and minerals, and so forth, that we need. His idea of a delicious meal may be different from ours, but his nutritional needs are the same.

Let's see what these needs are.

* On the other hand, it has also been pointed out that due to a lack of mechanical equipment, most farm work in LDCs is done by hand. Therefore the average Asian farmer probably could use more, not less, food energy than the average American farmer, and certainly more than the average American.

2

Human Food Requirements

A CAR LEFT OUT in the street will eventually turn into a pile of glass, steel, and plastic.

A pile of steel, glass, and plastic left out in the street will not eventually turn into a car.

A rock left out in the desert will eventually turn into a pile of sand.

A pile of sand left out in the desert will not eventually turn into a rock.

Why? Because a car is a more highly organized state of matter than a pile of glass, steel, and plastic, and because a rock is a more highly organized state than a pile of sand.

Something must cause the materials to form into a car or a rock; some organizing force must act on them, and some energy must be applied to make these things happen. This is because all things in the universe tend to move from the more- to the less-organized state.

Life has been called an exception to this natural law. A frog is obviously more complex than the single egg cell from which it grows. But even life is not an exception. For life, like other manufacturing or organizing processes, needs an external energy input to keep it from running down.

In plants, which constitute one major form of life (the other is animal life), that energy input is provided by the sun. But man eats plants, and he eats animals that in turn depend upon plants. Therefore the sun is ultimately the basic energy input for man and for all other animal species as well.

The Energy in Food

The close connection between the sun's energy and the energy we obtain from the food we eat is also seen in the use of the term *calorie*. Though the term is familiar to all, and especially weight-watchers, it is probable that not one person in a hundred understands its actual meaning.

A useful way to look at the situation is to consider the food we eat as a fuel, and our bodies as engines which can convert this fuel into both heat and work. Indeed, the body in a very real sense is "burning" this fuel, which is the main reason we need oxygen. (It is doing the very same thing an engine does, which is to convert the chemical energy stored in fuels into useful forms such as heat and/or mechanical energy, electricity, or what have you.) The burning of one pound of coal, it has been found, produces just about the amount of energy a man needs for one day's activities.

In physics, a calorie is defined as the amount of heat needed to raise the temperature of one gram of water one degree centigrade. (For fairly obvious reasons, those who do scientific work in nutrition think in metric terms; so we shall too. There are 28.35 grams to the ounce, and 454 to the pound.) But the calorie turns out to be an inconveniently small unit in the field of nutrition, and so the kilocalorie, or 1000 calories, is more often used. It is written in scientific papers as *kcal*. It is often called the large calorie, however, or simply calorie, which causes considerable confusion. To

30

prevent this we shall capitalize the word thus—*Calorie*—when we mean kcal.

So when we say that the average American takes in some 3000 Calories (or 3 million small calories), we are saying that this amount of food, if burned, could raise the temperature of 3000 *Kilo*grams of water one degree centigrade. Such a measurement is actually made in a process called calorimetry. One method is to place a known weight of a particular food in a closed metal container, called a bomb, along with some oxygen. The bomb is then put into a weighed amount of water, and the "fuel"—or food—is ignited electrically. The rise in temperature of the water is then measured.

The major use of the calorie concept in nutrition is to tell us how much energy a given amount of a particular food makes available. When we say that a tablespoon of honey contains 100 Calories, we mean that when "burned" (oxidized) in the body it will release that amount of energy for heat or the performance of work.

If you would like a better feeling for the numbers involved, think in terms of the watt. This is a familiar term in electrical equipment such as light bulbs and electric appliances; it is a measure of the *rate* at which energy is being used. A 70-watt bulb uses up energy at the rate of about one Calorie per minute.

This is roughly the rate at which a person's body uses up energy when he is resting in bed. In other words, there is a great deal going on in the body—breathing, heartbeat, digestion, and so on—even when a person is sleeping. Slow walking raises this figure to 180 watts and fast walking to 380.

One also uses more energy in a cold climate than in a warm one. Hence a lumberjack in action in the north woods may call upon his energy supply at the rate of 1,000 watts (14 Calories per minute) for short periods. The same is true for very energetic sports.

By figuring out the body's energy needs over the course of a day, we can get an idea of how much food is needed. (Some wise guy is bound to say, "You don't have to go through all of that. All you have to do is eat when you're hungry." But if that were true, then there would be no fat or skinny people, would there?) The caloric requirement for humans ranges from 1,500 to 4,000 Calories, with smaller, less active women at one end and men doing heavy manual labor in cold weather at the other. Excess food which is not used up by the body for energy, repair, growth, etc., can be converted by the body into fat and stored that way.

Human muscles are about 25 per cent efficient. This means that they are able to convert about 25 per cent of the energy contained in food to useful energy. The rest is given off as heat energy. (That is why you become overheated during strenuous physical activity.) Toward the end of the eighteenth century, when Benjamin Thompson* began to put some order into the food/energy question, mechanical engines (such as steam engines) were less efficient than this. And so Thompson concluded that prison labor was a cheaper energy source than mechanical engines!

No matter how much, or how little, food and water your body takes in, a roughly equivalent amount of solid and liquid waste leaves your body. Perhaps, then, you will wonder where the energy used by the body comes from. Isn't some of the food converted to energy? The answer is no. Rather the body is using energy already stored or locked up in food.

The food energy appears as chemical bonds, stored by plants in the process of building up their tissues. That is the energy we extract when our bodies go to work on the food. In the first stage the food is broken down into simpler components such as sugar molecules, fatty acids, and amino acids. The energy that had originally been taken from the sun's light

* Also known as Count Rumford.

is now made available to the human or animal body when it breaks these bonds. As a rough analogy, think of a spring-wound mechanical car. If it has an off-on switch you can wind it up and leave it on the floor; if the switch is on "off" it will just sit there. But touch the switch and the stored energy is suddenly made available.

The components into which the food is broken down can also be used to reconstruct parts of the body for growth, repair, and so on.

Food Requirements

Because of the tremendous complexity of the job done by our bodies, a great variety of substances must be taken in. It is estimated that some forty to forty-five elements and compounds are essential for good health and sound bodies. These fall into five general categories: carbohydrates, fats, protein, vitamins and minerals. Each is found in a large variety of foods, but no one food contains them all. This is important and explains the need to eat a "balanced meal," i.e., a meal that contains all the essential nutrients.

Broadly speaking, carbohydrates (such as sugar and starch) are used for energy. Fats serve as reservoirs of energy, but they are also used by the body as a construction material, as in the sheathing for nerves. Protein, however, is the main construction material. Vitamins, though present in very small amounts in the body, are vital to proper functioning, while minerals are also used in "construction," e.g., calcium in bones and teeth.

A 160-pound man is made up approximately of the following (in pounds): water, 100; protein, 29; fat, 25; minerals, 5; carbohydrates, 1; and vitamins, ½ *ounce*. Lack of *any* of these nutrients can cause sickness and even death. It took a long

33

time before this was realized. During the era of sailing ships, before refrigeration, rations were often lacking in one or more of these nutrients. Only those foods could be taken along that would not spoil over long periods of time. This meant that certain "basic" foods were lacking in the diet. Sickness was therefore a common passenger on the sometimes year-long sailings.

Perhaps you have come across the expression "limey" for a British sailor. This came about when the British admiralty finally realized that the very serious malady called scurvy, suffered by many sailors and characterized by weakness, pain, and internal bleeding, could be prevented by including limes in the diet of the men. (Hence "limey.") It was later realized that lack of vitamin C was causing the problem and that limes and other citrus fruits supply it in the diet. Though only the tiniest amount is needed, it is, as many unfortunate sailors found out, indeed necessary.

Vitamin C is interesting in another way. Many of the nutrients can be stored by the body. Thus if you eat more than you need, the body will store what is left over. Vitamin C cannot be stored and so the diet must contain a daily, or almost daily, ration of the foods that contain it.

At least a dozen vitamins are necessary in the human diet. A few of these, such as thiamine, niacin, and riboflavin, also cannot be stored. Nor can protein! Excess protein is converted to fat and is stored in that form. And, conversely, if not enough calories are available, proteins may be used to make up the deficit in order to keep the body running.

The average American gets less than half his energy (47 per cent) from carbohydrates; 41 per cent comes from fats and about 12 per cent from protein. In LDCs, as much as two-thirds of a person's energy requirements come from carbohydrates. Although rich in energy, carbohydrates are lacking in various other nutrients needed by the body.

34

Hunger vs. Malnutrition

We can now begin to get a better understanding of the difference between undernutrition (hunger) and malnutrition (not enough of the right kinds of foods).

In the first case there simply is not enough food of any kind. In India the average daily diet provides only about 1,700 calories; in Africa the figure is 2,000. The average requirement for a human being is thought to be in the range of 2,400. Men, being usually larger and doing heavier work, will need a few hundred more; women, a few hundred less.

When a person, and particularly an infant, does not receive enough food not only is he hungry but he is also weak and tired and has lowered resistance to disease. The problem is particularly acute for the very young, because that is their time of major growth. A large part of the problem is physical, because there is an actual shortage of food. But it is also at least partly a matter of ignorance. The poor mothers in LDCs, who often will try to copy the ways of the rich, may take their children off the breast at a very young age. But when they do this, they have no satisfactory substitute to feed the child, and he begins to suffer what is called marasmus. Such a child is thin and emaciated ("skin and bones"); he has wrinkled skin and large eyes. Many of the Biafran children, who suffered severe food shortages during their uprising against the Nigerians, show these symptoms.

You can imagine the reaction of a poor resident of an LDC let loose in one of our supermarkets. The profusion of foods might overwhelm him, but he would believe it. When, however, he got to the counter marked low-calorie, or diet foods, he would probably think he had taken leave of his senses. Who in his right mind would deliberately eat low-calorie foods? Yet production of these foods has become a major industry here.

35

Of course, for the American, whose average daily diet is more than 3,000 calories, it does make some sense. It would make more sense, however, for him to simply cut down on the intake of fatty meats, baked goods, rich sauces, and so on, while increasing the intake of fruits, vegetables, fish, lean meat, and poultry.

Proteins

Many of the LDCs are in warm climates. And, as we noted, many inhabitants of LDCs are smaller than the average Westerner. Hence their daily food requirements are probably actually lower than ours. But even if the LDC caloric and protein requirement is lower, the need for vitamins and other nutrients is about the same. It is usually figured that about .9 gram of protein is needed per kilogram of body weight per day. For a 100-pounder that comes to about 40 grams (roughly 1⅜ ounces) per day, while a 150-pounder would need 60 grams (about 2 ounces which could be provided by 10 ounces of meat or other protein food).

These figures, it should be mentioned, are not fixed numbers. Estimates for an average adult range all the way from a low of 40 grams to a high of 100 grams a day. Requirements vary, because of differences in size, growth, pregnancy, tissue repair due to injury, activity level, and so on. In addition, however, there are differences of opinion regarding even an average need for a given person. The interesting result is that a change of 10 grams in the accepted estimated requirement can suddenly make millions "malnourished."

But the fact remains that vast numbers of people throughout the world do not get even the lowest figure. The result is often a dreaded disease called *kwashiorkor*. We in the United States are fortunate in not hearing much about it,

36

Human Food Requirements

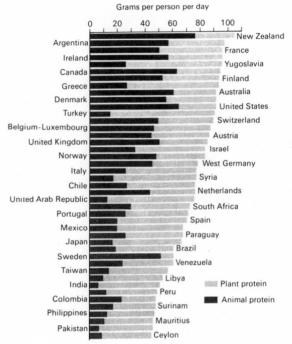

Grams per person per day

Daily per capita total protein supplies in 43 countries.

but it is common enough in the LDCs. P. R. and A. H. Ehrlich, in their book *Population, Resources, Environment,* provide this description of the disease:

Kwashiorkor is a West African word that means "the sickness the child develops when another baby is born." The sickness develops because the second child forces the first child off the breast. Kwashiorkor can occur even if calories are abundantly provided . . . In mild cases the child's physical growth is retarded, the hair and skin are discolored, and he has a pot-belly. He may also lose his appetite. When the disease is more acute, the discoloration is more pronounced, hair is loosely rooted and pulls out in tufts, legs and feet swell with fluids, digestive problems arise, and the child becomes mark-edly apathetic [uncaring]. After this stage is reached, death will follow unless the best medical care can be provided.

Nor have we come to the end of the protein problem in our discussion. There are thousands of different kinds of proteins in the body, all of which are made up of smaller constituents, or pieces, called *amino acids*. Strangely, there are only about twenty different amino acids; but they can combine in a multitude of different ways, and they do. The majority of these twenty can be manufactured in the body from simpler materials supplied by our foods. But eight cannot be gotten in any way except directly from the foods we eat. That is, they must be synthesized by plants and/or animals; our bodies cannot do this. These eight are therefore called the essential amino acids.

isoleucine	methionine	tryptophan
leucine	phenylalanine	valine
lysine	threonine	

The eight amino acids essential to the human diet.

Thus it is not only the amount of protein that counts. The makeup, or quality, of the protein is equally important. The meat of a chicken, for example, contains about 18 per cent protein. Feathers are made up of 86 per cent protein. While feathers are not the most appealing dish, if one is short of protein why doesn't he then grind up the feathers and somehow use all this protein? Aside from the taste problem, the amino acid balance is poor, lacking almost totally the essential amino aid tryptophan. Further, our digestive systems are not equipped to break down the tough fibrous materials in the feathers.

38

In general, the best balance of essential amino acids is found in meat and dairy foods. Green plants, especially the soybean, can supply them, but no single plant has been found to contain them all in any quantity. And since, as we shall see, in the LDCs the diet probably consists mainly of a single food grain such as rice or corn, with small additions of flavoring, the diet is very likely a deficient one. The result is that the poor in these areas can gorge themselves on their staple diet, yet still be deficient in various of the amino acids and perhaps other nutrients as well.

But meat and dairy foods are expensive, while the staple vegetables are not. There is a reason why this is so, and this makes up the substance of our next chapter.

3

Where Our Food Comes From

To THE AVERAGE AMERICAN, grass is something to be stepped on, to play football or baseball on, or perhaps to mow.

The farmer knows better.

There are at least a quarter of a million different plants found on earth. But the bulk of man's diet comes from just 12 grasses. These produce the so-called cereal grains—the dried seed-like fruit of cultivated grasses such as rice, wheat, corn, oats, rye, barley, sorghum, and millet.

The cereal grains are basic to man's diet today, particularly in the LDCs, and they have been throughout history. These plants are tough, develop a strong root system, and can grow in regions varying from hot to cold, wet to dry. They produce a lot of food per acre in comparison to other plants. They store relatively well and can therefore be transported easily. (Lettuce, for example, must be refrigerated or it quickly wilts.) And, finally, the grains are tasty and have a high caloric value.

Rice is the most important crop of all, the staple (basic) food for 60 per cent of all mankind. Probably 30 per cent of all human energy comes from rice. Rice, along with wheat and corn, accounts for fully half of all the cultivated land on earth.

Corn, native to the Americas, is still one of their most

important crops. It is the staple crop of South and Central
America, where it is eaten fresh and ground for flour. Corn
is an equally important crop in the United States, although
as much as three-quarters of it is used as animal feed. In
Europe this is practically the only use for corn. The production of corn oil, used for cooking, in margarine, etc., is
another important use.

In spite of the cereal grains' obvious usefulness, they are
not the perfect answer to human nutrition needs. One problem is that they are relatively low in proteins. In general,
beans and peas (legumes) contain two to four times as much
protein as the cereals. In many regions, therefore, where the
cost of meat takes it beyond the reach of the poor, the
legumes, when available and within economic reach, provide
most of the protein that is available. In Asia, legumes such
as soybeans, chickpeas, cowpeas, and string beans provide
20 per cent of all the protein that is eaten there.

But legumes (sometimes called *pulses*) provide another
advantage, which we will explore in the next two sections.

The Green Plant

The most important difference between plants and animals
is that plants are autotrophic, which literally means "self-
feeding." They are able, through the marvelous process
called photosynthesis, to take most of the elements they need
for their own cells out of the air and water and soil. Animals,
on the other hand, must get most of their carbohydrates, fats
and amino acids (for proteins) ready-made from plant or
other animal tissue.

The basic "ingredients" of all living things are carbon,
oxygen, hydrogen, and nitrogen, plus small amounts of a wide
variety of other elements, such as phosphorus, sulphur, and
iron. In photosynthesis, the plant cells are able to obtain their

carbon, oxygen, and hydrogen from the air and water around them, while the trace elements can generally be obtained from the soil, assuming they are there. It might help your understanding of what is happening if we put down the chemical formula for a basic sugar, glucose: $C_6H_{12}O_6$. As you can see, there are only three elements involved: carbon, hydrogen, and oxygen. Green plants obtain them from the carbon dioxide (CO_2) in the air around them and from water (H_2O). They can, in other words, manufacture this particular carbohydrate, and others which are similar, with the aid of the sun's energy. Fortunately, there is a virtually unending supply of these elements.

As mentioned, however, other minerals and trace elements are needed for proper growth and functioning of the plant cells. The table shows the minerals withdrawn from soil by 1,000 pounds of maize (Indian corn). Lack of any one of them can clamp a limit on the speed or amount of growth of the plant.

ELEMENT	LBS.
Nitrogen	22.3
Potassium	14.6
Calcium	14.1
Phosphorus	3.7
Magnesium	3.6
Sulphur	2.3
Zinc	0.044
Manganese	0.022
Copper	0.010

Minerals withdrawn from soil by 1,000 pounds of maize.

The major problem here is that these elements are not automatically replenished, as are the air and water. At least not any more. In the old days, when humans as well as their domesticated animals often lived in the same place as that from which they were taking their food, then the elements of which they were composed went back into the soil when they died.

Today that is no longer true. More and more we are living in urban areas which are quite separated from the place where plants are grown or livestock raised. Hence very few of the elements removed from one area are automatically put back into that area.

Further, the amount of plant life that was grown in early days was small. And so, relatively few of the soil nutrients were removed. If too much was taken out, and the farmer saw that the productivity of the land was dropping, he simply moved his attentions to a different place. The land was allowed to "lie fallow" for a while, to give it time to regain some of its "strength."

Today of course we can no longer do that. There are no longer unending acres of fertile land just waiting to be put under the plow. Most of the good land, especially that with plenty of natural moisture available, has been under cultivation for quite a while. Further, increasing population has required that much more food be grown in the same amount of land. (In other parts of the world, the problem is compounded.)

The answer to the problem of the fertile land deficit, as I am sure you have guessed, is fertilizer. The whole point of fertilizer is to replace those elements that have been removed by cultivation and not returned to the soil afterwards. Nutrients may also be lost from the soil through erosion (loss of topsoil), or the nutrients may actually dissolve ("leach") out of the soil if too much water runs through the soil, or if the water doesn't drain away properly.

Although fertilization is not the only thing that must be done to keep the soil in good shape, it is certainly one of the most important.

More and more chemical or mineral fertilizer is being used. This means that the elements themselves, such as nitrogen, phosphorus and potassium, are added directly to the soil, though they are carried as part of chemical compounds which aid in delivery of the elements. This type of fertilizer is also called inorganic or artificial.

The term *inorganic* is an interesting one. It was once thought that there were two basic kinds of material: organic (living) and inorganic (nonliving). Skin, for instance, was thought to be an organic material, while rock was inorganic.

Plants clearly are organic matter. And it had been seen that plants grew taller or faster in the presence of animal manure, which probably led to the idea of fertilizer. So animal manure would be spread, or bone or fish meal; a mixture of decaying leaves and other ex-living things also seemed to help.

Thus the idea grew, and still remains among many adherents to the "organic" or "health food" method of agriculture, that only organic or "natural" fertilizers should be used. Chemical fertilizers are supposedly poisonous or in some way detrimental to the food.

What is not generally realized is that when organic fertilizer is put on or in soil, all that happens is that soil bacteria break it down and release the chemical elements so that they can be utilized by the plants. The end result of organic or inorganic fertilization is exactly the same, at least as far as the soil nutrients are concerned. Organic fertilizer may help to physically "condition" the soil. But that is another matter.

This is not to say that chemical pesticides may not be harmful. But these should definitely not be confused with chemical fertilizers.

44

The first realization that organic and inorganic materials were different only in their chemistry came early in the nineteenth century. Urea, until then produced only by animals and found in urine, was clearly an organic substance. But imagine the consternation of the organic/life adherents when the German chemist Friedrich Wöhler created the material in his laboratory!

So a new distinction had to be made between the terms organic and inorganic, as in organic and inorganic chemistry. That distinction, from a scientific point of view, became, and still is, that organic chemistry is concerned with those materials that contain carbon.

Now, it is true that carbon, which has the ability to combine in many ways with other elements, is the basic component of the large, highly complex molecules found in living things. On the other hand, carbon is also found in carbon dioxide, which can hardly be called a living thing. The distinction between organic and inorganic matter still baffles many people.

Nitrogen Fixation

Fortunately, as we mentioned earlier, plants are able to obtain their carbon from the carbon dioxide in the air. But now we come to an interesting problem. Fats and carbohydrates are composed mainly of carbon, hydrogen, and oxygen, all of which are commonly available. Proteins, however, contain an additional element, nitrogen. So do the nucleic acids that have been found to be the crucial conveyors of our heredity.

But, ironically, although nitrogen makes up 78 per cent of our atmosphere, the cereal grasses cannot take up ("fix") nitrogen from the air. They must obtain it from nitrogen compounds, chiefly nitrates. So, although there is an unlimited quantity of this important element in the atmosphere, these plants must obtain it from another source.

The nitrogen can come from one or more of only three sources. First there is the reuse of biological substances containing nitrogen, as when manure is used as fertilizer. Again, this worked well when the pressures to produce were not as great as they are now, and when production was not as highly organized as it is now. For example, when cows were allowed to graze at will, their manure was automatically spread around at random. Today cows are often housed and fed in large cow sheds or in densely populated feed lots. Their manure then becomes a waste that must be disposed of. As a matter of fact, agricultural wastes are the number one solid-waste disposal problem in the United States today.

The second way that plants can obtain their nitrogen is through chemical fertilizers, which we have already discussed. The quantities of nitrogen used in various parts of the world vary enormously. Professor N. W. Pirie, a British biochemist, reports that Japan, Western Europe, Latin America, and tropical Africa and India use 300, 160, 16, and 2 pounds of nitrogen respectively for each cultivated acre.

Because nitrogen does not combine easily with other elements, it must be driven, dragged, or otherwise caused to go into combination with something else, such as hydrogen or oxygen, before it can be used by plants. When done artificially, the process is called *industrial fixation*, though it is actually the manufacture of nitrate, and it has an interesting aspect. Most industrial methods require an energy input of about 16 million calories (16,000 kcal) per pound of nitrogen fixed. Lightning, for example, can cause fixation of nitrogen, but we can hardly depend upon that for a regular supply. This means that the energy input requirement for nitrates can amount to as much as 10 per cent of the energy that will eventually be obtained from the entire crop! And energy is expensive. Is it any wonder that nitrates and other chemical fertilizers are not readily available in the LDCs?

In both of the above-mentioned methods, the plant takes up nitrogen from the soil in the form of a nitrate. There are some plants however that can take up the element directly from the air. They do this with the aid of nitrogen-fixing bacteria that live in, or in association with, the plant's roots! Actually, the nitrogen-fixing bacteria are using the atmospheric nitrogen to manufacture their own proteins. Because the bacteria are so closely associated with the plant, these materials can then be taken up by the plant. This process is called *biological fixation.*

The legumes, e.g., peas and beans, have this ability. As a result, they are often called "green manure," for when ploughed back into the ground (after the useful parts have been harvested), the final result is more nitrogen in the soil than there was before these plants were sowed. Other plants, such as alfalfa, are also useful in this way. Sometimes farmers therefore rotate their crops to take advantage of this type of natural fertilization.

The word "plant," by the way, also means a place where things are manufactured. This second meaning undoubtedly grew out of the verb *to plant,* which means "to set firmly in or on the ground." But the double use has more meaning than you may think. It has been estimated that each year the process of photosynthesis converts 200 billion tons of atmospheric carbon to sugar. This is about 100 times the combined weight of all the things man produces in that time.

While grains and legumes comprise the bulk of man's vegetable food supply, there are dozens of other plant foods that are important in various parts of the world. Potatoes, sweet potatoes, and cassava (a cactus-like plant) supply starch to many peoples, while the sugar beet and cane sugar plants supply sugar. Various parts of green plants may be consumed, like the stem of the celery, the leaves of spinach, or the root of the carrot. All provide various vitamins and minerals that are needed for good health. Fruits, berries and nuts round out the vegetable diets of peoples around the world.

Food From Animals

Many plants are useless to humans but provide fine feed for animals. Alfalfa and clover, both legumes, and many grasses fall into this category. Some of the plants consumed by animals are wild. But again, with the pressures of mounting population, the meat industry must be put on a firmer, more controlled foundation, and so a great deal of the animal feed must be grown on farms. We already mentioned the importance of corn; alfalfa is also a very important feed crop. Some 60 million acres of land are used for this crop around the world.

There is both good and bad in this picture—that is, using good farmland to grow food for animals, and then using the animals as human food.

On the good side is the fact that animal food generally contains a better balance of proteins for humans than does vegetable food. There are ways of getting around this, as is evidenced by a fairly large number of vegetarians (by choice or necessity) around the world. But the vegetable diet must be carefully balanced, or else not enough of certain kinds of protein will be taken in. An unbalanced diet leads to malnourishment in the face of apparent plenty.

Roger Revelle, food and population expert, tells us that farmers in the United States produce an average of 11,000 Calories per person per day. From this, we use about 2,000 directly for our food needs; we export 2,000; and we feed

7,000 to livestock (cattle, pigs, chickens, turkeys, etc.). From this 7,000 Calories we get back the additional 1,000 needed to fill out the average American's 3,000-Calorie diet. In other words, it takes an average of about seven Calories of feed crop to produce one Calorie of meat, milk, or eggs. This is the negative side of the picture.

We shall see later that attempts are being made to reduce this ratio. For example, urea is being included in cows' rations in place of some of the protein they normally need, and poultry droppings can provide up to one-third of a pig's protein needs. Both urea and the chicken droppings are high in nitrogen and can be blended into the feed crop with no apparent objections from the animals.

Animals can be thought of as protein factories which use plant food as raw materials. And, like any type of factory, some are more efficient than others. Beef seems to be the most highly preferred form of meat; but cows are, unfortunately, among the more inefficient producers. As can be seen in the table, their conversion efficiency (the ratio of plant protein

ANIMAL PRODUCT	CONVERSION EFFICIENCY (PER CENT)
Steer, beef	7
Pig, pork	17
Chicken	23
Hen, eggs	36
Cow, milk	47

Conversion efficiency of plant to food protein.

taken in to that given back) is only 7 per cent. Production of milk is a more efficient method, with almost half the food intake being turned into milk, while chickens can turn about a quarter of their food intake into meat.

Cows, however, have an important capability. As members of the group called *ruminants* they have a special chamber in their stomachs, the rumen, in which microorganisms in their systems can convert non-protein nitrogen into the amino acids they need. Thus they can subsist on plants that are useless to us. These microorganisms combine the nitrogen and carbohydrates taken in by the cattle to form protein. The cattle can then use this protein since it is being produced in their own digestive system. Sheep also have this ability, although pigs, chickens and other non-ruminants do not. Nor does man; remember that eight amino acids are essential to the human diet (See page 38). It should be mentioned, however, that two Cornell scientists have recently reported experiments indicating that chickens and Japanese quail can convert the chemical diammonium citrate into protein. Therefore, say the scientists, this chemical could replace part of the protein in the diet of chickens.

Be that as it may, this ability makes cows able to take chemical urea in their fodder. With this addition, the conversion efficiency figure goes up to 70 per cent for milk and 17 per cent for beef. Although a considerable improvement, this is still less than one-fifth of the food intake being returned as meat. But, beef and milk production remain a very important part of the American diet, as is shown by a calculation of Dr. James Bonner of the California Institute of Technology. He figures that there is three times as great a weight of cows in the United States as people.

Compared to growing vegetables, therefore, the care and feeding of animals is an inefficient way to obtain protein. One of the problems of course is that cows, pigs and chickens are living things and, like us, they need food energy to perform their daily functions as well as to put on weight for

50

our pleasure. Or, to put it another way, they exhale most of their food value in the form of carbon dioxide!

The DCs are fortunate in being able to afford this kind of waste. For a hungry world, however, serious problems arise from increasing the number of animals to increase the food supply. Even in the United States, meat is the most expensive part of a meal, both in cost to the consumer and use of arable land.

Other solutions will have to be found, including finding new ways of using existing foods and creating altogether new ones. We shall talk about these developments later in the book. A more important approach, at least for the near future, is to increase the quality as well as the quantity of vegetable protein. We shall see in the next few chapters that methods for improving both are being investigated.

One way to increase quantities is to put more land under cultivation. Let's see first what that entails.

4

Labor, Land, and Land Substitutes

JOAQUIN CASTELLANOS IS A Mexican who lives in the state of Puebla, about 100 miles northeast of Mexico City. He could be considered one of the lucky ones, for he owns 10 acres of land in this agricultural region. Yet, like many of his neighbors, he tried for years but couldn't seem to make the land pay off. In 1967 his total cash income was the equivalent of $128.

The following year he simply gave up. He rented the land to a neighbor and moved to Mexico City to try to make a living there—if one can call a job as construction worker at $20 a month a living. Still, it was the best he could do. To make things worse, his wife and children had to be left behind at the farm.

Señor Castellanos is neither stupid nor lazy. What then was the problem?

Corn is the dominant crop in this region. But yields have traditionally been so low that the farmers often could not even grow enough for their own table, let alone produce an excess which they could sell to obtain money for other needs.

Fortunately for Señor Castellanos and other farmers in the area, Puebla was chosen as a "test case" in a program to see

Some dubious Puebla farmers need more convincing than others.

whether technical assistance by experts could help increase the corn yields. The Puebla Project was conceived and organized by the International Maize and Wheat Improvement Center (CIMMYT or Centro International de Mejoramiento de Maíz y Trigo) located in Mexico City and funded by the Rockefeller and Ford Foundations in the United States.

The first problem, strangely enough, was to get the local officials to support the project. They were as skeptical as the farmers who "had tried everything."

After some investigation the experts came up with some recommendations. The first thing that was needed, they said, was more credit; and it should be made available to the farmers in March rather than the traditional May. Although the farmers had been using fertilizer, they had been applying it at the later date rather than at planting time. Because of this, very little of the phosphorus in the fertilizer reached the root zone in time to help the crop.

Soil research showed that the farmers were wasting their money in adding potash to the soil. Potash is potassium carbonate, a common fertilizing substance. What the farmers had no way of knowing was that there was plenty of this substance already available in the local volcanic soils.

The Puebla farmers had traditionally spread about 6,000 to 10,000 seeds per acre, by dropping seeds with every step. The CIMMYT experts figured this could be doubled and that seeds could be dropped at every half step.

Over 140 farmers had been signed up for the project, and demonstration plots were set up. Neighbors were invited in at intervals to observe new techniques, like mixing and spreading of fertilizer. Toward the end of the season farmers from a wide area were invited to see the results.

And the results were worth seeing. In all cases the yields were double, triple, and even quadruple what had been obtained before.

Señor Castellanos' story has a happy ending. He heard about the project from a neighbor, and on a visit home saw for himself what was happening. He is now back on his beloved land. In addition to being able to feed his family he expects to bring in twice as much money as he was making in the city. And he can stay on the land, where he feels he belongs.

Even more important, perhaps, is the fact that a food-poor region began to move toward self-sufficiency.

An important lesson is illustrated in this story. One cannot take the developments that have worked in the advanced areas of the world and simply transport them to the LDCs. Each area presents its own set of problems and will require its own set of answers. Tractors, for example, have done wonders in the United States. Why, then, it is often thought,

Improvements in yield enabled Joaquin Castellanos to return from the slums of Mexico City to his own farm.

wouldn't they do the same in the LDCs? And so, many LDC governments have bought tractors. But at any one time in a given LDC, fully half the tractors may lie idle because of lack of spare parts or because maintenance is not available. And money that might have been spent on more fertilizer or better seed or in a hundred other ways lies tied up in machinery that cannot be used.

A "New" Approach

It is worth noting that the Puebla Project approach to increasing food production is relatively new in world history. Traditionally, increases in food production have been accomplished by simply putting more land under the plow. Clearly, though, with ever increasing populations this cannot continue; there are areas, such as Japan, where virtually all the arable land is being farmed. Thus it is no surprise that Japan was the first country to institute the first real change that increased food production. The Japanese have succeeded in increasing the yield per acre. The area of cultivated land in Japan reached a peak in 1920, and has decreased considerably since then, while food production has continued to rise.

The situation is similar in most of the DCs, where land use for farming has remained relatively steady or has actually declined in the past twenty to thirty years. In the LDCs, however, this is not so; the major food production increases have continued to come from converting additional land areas to farming.

The total land area of the world is some 7 billion acres. Of this perhaps 3 billion is being used to produce food. Those who would tell us that there is no population problem point to this other land and say there is still plenty of land available. Indeed, much of this land is underpopulated, they say. True. But maybe there are very good reasons why it is

Crop production per acre and crop land used, United States, 1870–1965.

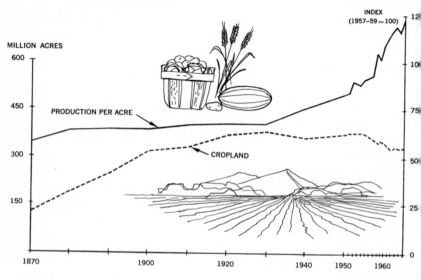

underpopulated: much of this land does not have enough water, or is too cold, or too hot, or is unlivable for any of a dozen other reasons. There is plenty of land available in the middle of the United States, for example. But getting water to it is an enormously expensive process. Some have suggested that we build an enormous canal from northern Canada!

Land Problems

Many tropical areas have plenty of water. But you can take all the usual ideas about a lush tropical jungle and its promise as a good place to farm and throw them out.

D. Luis Bramao, a United Nations soil expert, tells of an experience he had which illustrates this very well. In 1965 he was traveling through Brazil, mainly to study the soil resources of the region. Along the way he stopped at a farm being run by a Texan who had moved down there. The American told Señor Bramao that he had put eight years of hard work into the farm and had sunk all his savings into equipment for clearing the land. His idea was to create a huge, modern farm of the type found in the United States. Land was cheap, and there was even a good road which had been built to connect the new capital, Brasilia, to the more populated coastal region.

There was only one problem, which Señor Bramao hadn't the heart to tell the Texan. "For this man," he says, "we had arrived too late." The problem? The forest had "kept together the poor, exhausted land that made up his property. By clearing it, he had turned it into a desert."

The wealth of a good agricultural region is found in its soil; in tropical jungles this wealth is found in the lushness of the vegetation. As the plants and trees die, the nutrients

A tropical rain forest is no place to grow food—for the present.

locked up in their trunks, leaves, stalks and roots go back to the soil to be recycled. Clear all of this away, and there is very little left.

One cannot ignore the lessons taught by nature. The type of vegetation that grows naturally must be studied, for it has adapted to special conditions. In the wet tropics that special condition is too much water! And too much can be just as serious as too little.

Not only can plants become waterlogged and even drown in waterlogged soil, but the constant movement of water through the soil tends to drain or leach away the nutrients. This is why the jungle makes sense in the tropics; the lush vegetation keeps the nutrients "in storage," and prevents them from being washed away!

What the Texan had done was a repeat of experiences had by civilizations the world over. As long as there were few

58

people and much land, this was not too great a problem. One simply moved away. Many dead towns, villages and even cities are left to tell the tale. There are 100 such cities and villages in Syria alone. North Africa was once a fertile area and produced the grain for the great Roman Empire. It is now largely desert.

What happens is that the land loses its fertility and plants are no longer able to grow there. This would be bad enough. But without a green cover, wind and rain begin to blow or wash away the upper layers of soil. In a matter of a few years, the topsoil which has taken hundreds or even thousands of years to build up is blown or washed away, leaving a useless, dead area that is of no value to anyone. Each year, reports A. H. Boerma,* soil erosion causes the abandoning of millions of acres of crop land in Asia, the Middle East, North Africa, and Central America. The Sahara desert is said to be advancing south along a broad front at a rate of several miles a year.

In some areas, depending upon the constitution of the natural soil, a complex chemical process may turn it into a clay-like surface. The process by which this happens is called *laterization*, and the result is laterite, a hard raw surface that is practically useless and almost impossible to cultivate. Thus it is that inhabitants of lush tropical jungle regions may be among the worst fed in the world.

Nor is crop farming the only culprit. In some areas of eastern Africa herds of livestock have been allowed to overgraze. As a result the natural grasses, which were at one time stable and nutritious the year round, have disappeared. Depending on how bad the conditions are, the grasses may be replaced by small useless weeds that come and go, by useless brush, or even by bare earth. The tsetse fly begins to

* Director-General of the Food and Agriculture Organization (FAO) of the U.N.

multiply enormously and the region rapidly becomes uninhabitable for animal and man.

So most of the additional food for at least the immediate future will have to come from present day farm lands.

"Substitutes" for Land

Fortunately, there are a number of different approaches which, used alone or together, act as "substitutes" for land. High yielding crops, irrigation, use of crops better suited for the particular soil or climate involved, scientific farming, chemical fertilizers, control of diseases, pests and rodents, and greater mechanization are among the various methods that are or can be used.

One ton of nitrogen, for instance, is said to be the equivalent of 14 acres of good farmland. It has been estimated that without fertilizers 50 per cent more land would be needed to produce what is produced today, and food costs would obviously be much higher. A great deal can be done along these lines to increase yields in the LDCs, which now use only about a fifth of the world production of fertilizer. Nor is the United States the most intensive user; the Japanese farmer uses twice as much fertilizer as his counterpart in the United States. This of course ties in with the shortage of land in Japan. The use of fertilizer has increased world-wide over the past decade at an average rate of 12 per cent.

Although fertilizer will increase production when used alone, it is usually best to combine it with one or more of the other "substitutes" for land we mentioned earlier, and with others we have yet to discuss.

Japan and the United States are both very efficient food producers, but in different ways. Japan has a higher output per acre on the average. But theirs is a labor-intensive

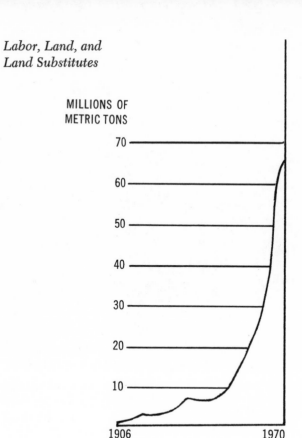

MILLIONS OF
METRIC TONS

Total world consumption of chemical fertilizers.

method; they use a great deal of hand labor. The United States, on the other hand, has a higher output per farmer. Indeed only about five to seven per cent of the United States population produces enough food for the rest of the population, with much to spare. However, when related "agri-businesses" are included, e.g., tractor production, food distribution, etc., then as much as one-third of the U.S. labor force may be involved. This makes the overall food industry by far the largest in the country.

Let's look at the farming situation another way. A hundred years ago the average American farmer produced enough

The new little Ford tractor costs the same as a pair of oxen.

food and fiber for six other people. Today he produces enough for thirty to forty others. And by the year 2000 he is expected to produce enough for anywhere from 60 to 150 others.

Thanks to this remarkable production record, Americans have (or can have, if they eat properly) the best diet in the world, while spending the lowest percentage of their income for it. *International Harvester Farm* magazine reports that food takes only about 17 per cent of the American dollar, but that it takes 30 per cent of the British consumer's income, and 45 per cent of the Russian's.

A major factor has been mechanization. It is not generally realized that as recently as the 1930's there were still far more horses than tractors on our farms. A Dupont scientist has calculated that in the United States alone, farmers move 600 billion tons of soil per year, as they plow, cultivate, drain, and grade land. The use of machines shortens the time spent on each of these processes; but it does something else that is very important. Plowing a field is very tough work. It takes a lot of energy. That energy has to be paid for somehow. If people do it, they will eat more. When farm animals were put to the task, they increased the work output greatly; but they also ate more. A major advantage of mechanization is that it releases food for people which was formerly required to feed animals.

It has been estimated that the present day feeding requirements for animal power are still as much as two-thirds (in terms of energy) as those for people. It is not necessarily the same food, of course, but land is released for growing human food when mechanization is increased.

Unfortunately, almost 95 per cent of the tractors in use in the world are found in the more advanced countries. To help the process of mechanization get moving in the LDCs, Ford has just developed a small, unusual-looking tractor that is simple to use and easy to maintain. It costs roughly the same as a pair of bullocks, yet is expected to have twice the productivity. And of course it does not have to be fed with substances that, directly or indirectly, take food away from human mouths.

5

Agricultural Research

PROFESSOR N. W. PIRIE, food expert and biochemist, points out that: "The improvement of agriculture has always depended on two factors: the systematization and application of old experience and the acquisition of new knowledge." It is not generally known that the great production feat of American (and other DC) agriculture is largely a result of the second factor, research. S. H. Wittwer, agricultural expert at Michigan State University, points out that only within the last twenty-five to thirty years have crop yields increased substantially in the United States.

At the heart of the research system have been the so-called land-grant colleges established under the Morrill Act of 1862. From these have grown many of the great state colleges and universities of today, some of which still include the A & M in their names—for agricultural and mechanical. Today a number of these institutions are closely tied in with the U.S. Department of Agriculture through the maintenance of Agricultural Experiment Stations in various parts of the country.

As with the Puebla Project, the establishment of *local* research institutions, which could be concerned with local conditions and problems, made all the difference. The Univer-

Agricultural
Research

sity of Illinois, for instance, has been concerned with the problems of agriculture in the Great Plains, while the Agricultural Experiment Station at the University of Alaska is concerned with the special problems found there. Roscoe Taylor, a plant scientist at the station, points out that a certain barley may produce a high yield under good growing conditions, but it would have little value in the Palmer, Alaska, area where wind might completely ruin the crop by "shattering" it.

Naturally, research in an organized fashion did not take place immediately upon passage of the Morrill Act, or even upon creation of the land grant colleges. It takes time for this kind of thing to get going: faculty and scientists must be recruited; there must be experiments, which may take years to complete; there must be interchange of results; and there has to be a change in attitude toward the scientific approach and a general belief that science can help. Without this, students will not enter the field, nor will there be money to support it. Agriculture thus finally became a science in the sense that we know it today. Indeed, Miss Carolyn D.

An experiment in progress at the University of Minnesota's Agricultural Experiment Station, where work is being done with a substance that enables some plants to survive the state's subzero winters.

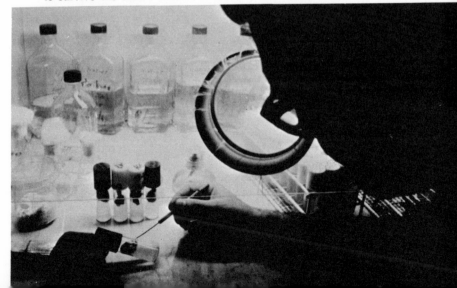

Hay, in her master's thesis "A History of Science Writing in the United States," maintains that the first regular science column in the United States was a weekly discussion of scientific agriculture in the *New York Tribune*, starting in 1870.

Nevertheless, because of this time lag organized research in plant science didn't take place until the end of the nineteenth century, while that in animal science didn't get under way until the beginning of the twentieth. And the results were even slower to show up.

PLANT OR ANIMAL AND FOODSTUFF				AVERAGE YIELD	RECORD YIELD
Corn—	bu./acre/year			80 (USA)	304
Wheat—	”	”	”	29 (USA)	209
Rice—	”	”	”	24 (World)	266
Oats—	”	”	”	53 (USA)	297
Grain sorghum—	”	”	”	56 (USA)	347
Soybeans—	”	”	”	27 (USA)	95
Potatoes—	”	”	”	350 (USA)	1,400
Sugarcane—tons sugar/ acre/year				2 (World)	5.5
Milk—lbs./cow/year				8,800 (USA)	15,000
Eggs—no./chicken/year				230 (USA)	365

Some average and record yields of crops and other foodstuffs.

But show up they did, and by 1940, we began to see rapid improvement in many areas. Yields of corn remained at 22 to 26 bushels per acre for almost a century and a half (1800–

66

Agricultural Research

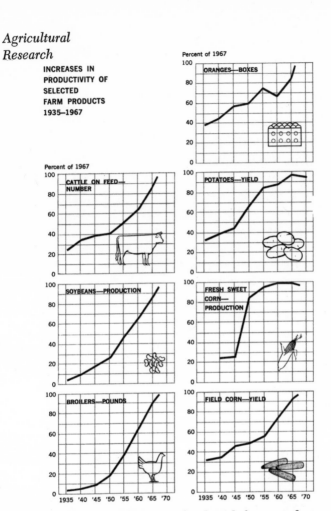

INCREASES IN
PRODUCTIVITY OF
SELECTED
FARM PRODUCTS
1935–1967

Increases in productivity of selected farm products.

1940). Since then, however, yields of corn and potatoes have more than tripled, while those for soybeans and wheat have doubled. And the improvement in yields continues. It is hoped that a similar improvement in yield, which is just beginning to happen in the LDCs, can be maintained.

An important part of the research job is to show how much can be produced on an acre of land. The chart shows average yield as opposed to record yield for a number of crops. As you can see, the difference is quite substantial. Also, the fact that something can be done on one experimental acre does not mean that it can be done on a large scale or even that it is worth the effort involved. After a while, one reaches what is called the point of diminishing returns. This means, from an economic point of view, that you have to invest more (in terms of labor, time, money, and/or raw materials) than you get back from that investment.

On the other hand, it does give an indication of what can be done. In a letter to *Science* magazine R. B. Davis, a worker at an experimental farm in India, reported that "it is possible to grow at least ten times more food per acre than the average for this area on land which was considered so poor when we bought it that nobody wanted to cultivate it."

This would be an example of the "systematization and application of old experience." We turn now to research which, hopefully, will lead to the acquisition of new knowledge.

Chemicals

We usually think of chemicals only in terms of chemical pesticides and fertilizers, or perhaps as food additives. But various substances are proving useful in a number of other ways as well. It has been found, for example, that growth can be speeded up; as a result it may be possible to grow two or more crops where only one could be grown before. On the other hand it may be desirable to slow down growth, which may be a good idea in the face of cold weather or a long dry spell.

A substance called an *auxin* can induce flowering, resulting in the uniform development of fruits. This is clearly useful

A growth-regulating chemical helped these grapes
mature.

in mechanical harvesting of crops. It has even been found
that some plants can be helped to withstand periods of
stress (cold or drought) with the aid of certain chemicals.

Another example of what can be done: lettuce seed tends
not to sprout if the temperature is too high. For a plant
growing wild, this would be a good ("life-saving") characteristic. Heat in desert areas is normally associated with dry

periods; this characteristic would prevent the seed from sprouting in what would normally be a dry period. Under controlled conditions and irrigation, however, it unnecessarily limits production of the crop. In one experiment, lettuce seed immersed for a few minutes in a substance called KN or kinetin germinated (began to grow) at temperatures as high as 90°F.

Chemicals have been found that will keep apples on trees for a longer time, permitting them to grow larger, and others that keep them firmer for a longer period. Experiments have shown that chemical agents may be able to protect plants from frost, a serious and recurring threat in many areas.

Research, using radioactive chemicals as "tracers," has shown that plants take in water and nutrients through leaves as well as roots. Fertilizer is and will remain in very short supply in many regions. It may be that a higher efficiency of application can be developed through "foliar feeding"—applying the fertilizer directly to the leaves, instead of indirectly through the soil and roots.

Photosynthesis

Because photosynthesis is the foundation for our food supply, it seems reasonable that if a basic breakthrough in food production is to take place, it will be in this process. First, photosynthesis is inefficient in that it utilizes only a small percentage of the light falling on the plant. The figure for normal growth ranges around .1 to 1 per cent. With modern techniques the figure might go up to 3 to 8 per cent. Theoretically it might be brought up to 30 to 40 per cent.

How?

There are two basic ways. One involves the shape and color of the leaves, for here most of the photosynthetic process

70

takes place. Plastic corn plants of different shapes are being used to try to find the best shape of leaf and plant so as to utilize the greatest amount of sunlight. The normal shape of the plant has been that of a canopy or umbrella; this means the lower leaves do not receive much light. And without the sun's energy, photosynthesis cannot take place. Changes in the shape of the plant are being made so that it grows more like a pyramid; in this way all the leaves will receive as much sun as possible. Another possible shape is an upright, narrow leaf pattern which allows greater light penetration and higher planting densities.

The color of the leaves is also important. Darker leaves will absorb more sunlight, lighter ones less. However, the more sunlight is absorbed, the warmer the leaf gets and the more water it will need. What happens is that the heat of the sun evaporates water from the leaves and they are then drier (hopefully) than the roots. This causes movement of water up through the stalk which carries nutrients from roots to leaves where the manufacturing of carbohydrates takes place. The warming of the leaves also causes circulation of the air and brings more carbon dioxide to them. So clearly there are a number of factors to be considered.

A group working at the Lawrence Radiation Laboratory in California is experimenting with photosynthesis outside the plant cell. This will aid in understanding the process and perhaps make it more efficient. Another possibility is to find out how to make plants manufacture more protein and less carbohydrate.

A third approach of course, would be to learn how to make plants carry out the process under controlled, factory conditions. An interesting set of experiments, run with flashing lights at night, gives indication that the biological clocks of plants can be "reset" to regulate fruiting, flowering, and general development.

Pouring on the light increases yield.

Farm expert Johnny Pendleton of the University of Illinois says that a corn plant is like a factory, and that the more fuel a factory gets, the more work it can do. He claims that of all the various ways of getting plants to produce more and faster, the one that has worked best is pouring on more light. In one experiment, aluminum reflectors were placed at the sides of a row of plants to increase the sunlight shining on them. The result was an almost unbelievable rate of 377 bushels per acre. This was double the rate of the plants on inside rows and 50 per cent more than similar end rows without the reflectors. Clearly this is not a practicable method and was used only to prove a point. But from experiments such as these we may develop practical methods.

At what might be called the opposite end of the scale we find a group working at the Physical Research Center in California who is growing plants in the dark! It is substituting other kinds of radiation for light and has shown that plants can be grown this way; but so far the efficiencies (output per energy input) have been even lower than that of sun-grown plants.

Other factors that must be considered are the temperature, both of the air and the soil, and the concentration of carbon dioxide around the plant. It is known, for instance, that the rate of chemical reaction generally doubles for each temperature rise of 18°F. This means that the rate of growth of a plant will be higher in warm than in cold areas. But only up to a point. After that the rate of growth decreases. The figure varies for different plants, indicating that there is something, perhaps a chemical, that can regulate this maximum. Perhaps, if the right chemical is found it can be used to help grow certain useful plants that do not do well in the tropics. We may find that future farmers will heat their fields, much as they irrigate them now.

Prof. Robert B. Musgrave keeps a watchful eye on his leaf chamber, a device used in a study of the photosynthetic efficiency of corn plants. The results may lead to development of high-yielding corn varieties.

Corn has been found to be the most efficient converter of solar energy to food. An experimental cornfield has been set up in upper New York State which samples the air at various locations around a plant to check the levels of water vapor, carbon dioxide, and air temperature to get a better idea of what is happening both outside and inside the plant. Some have suggested increasing the level of carbon dioxide at the brightest part of the day, when photosynthesis is going on at the most rapid rate.

The Agricultural Experiment Station at the University of Minnesota points out that corn, and other larger-grain members of the grain (grass) family, fix carbon dioxide at twice the rate of small grain types like rice and wheat. They report too that one of their research teams has developed a way to measure the photosynthetic efficiency of small grains in a matter of minutes—a process that used to take weeks. Eventually, it is hoped, we can somehow give large-grain efficiency to the small grains.

Multiple Cropping

Another farm technique that is becoming increasingly important is multiple cropping. The traditional approach is to plant one grain crop a year. It has been shown, however, that with careful handling the land can produce two, three, and sometimes even four crops a year! In certain tropical regions with long dry and wet seasons, for example, drought-resistant sorghum can be alternated with thirsty rice. Wheat, which needs only about one-third as much water as rice, is another intercropping possibility.

And who says that we have to work on a yearly basis? The future farmer may very well begin to ignore the calendar

74

Multiple cropping experiment at the University of Arizona.

year. In places like Mysore, a state in southern India, the growing conditions are relatively stable. Here it has been shown that three crops can be grown in fourteen months. Until recently this could not be done because the crops were sensitive to the length of day—when days were too short they would not grow. As with the non-germination of the lettuce seeds, this was a kind of defense mechanism to prevent the plants from growing at a time when it was most likely that conditions were not conducive to survival.

Even more advanced is relay intercropping, planting the second crop before the first is harvested—in interspersed rows.

"In the long run," writes A. H. Boerma, "the possibility of increasing cropping intensities may be even more exciting than that of increasing yields."

But both approaches have come out of a basic change in agriculture: the development of new types of seed. Here the whole process of change begins. We talk more about this in the next chapter.

6

Genetic Engineering

IMAGINE A FARMER who happily surveys his field of rich, ripening grain one evening. Later on there is a heavy rain. The next morning he comes out and finds that a major proportion of his crop, weighed down by its own luxuriant growth, has fallen over. Nutrients can no longer flow through the broken stalks and the crop is ruined.

Under nature's growing conditions, such as occasional flooding and competition from weeds, the natural and best form for the plant might be tall and skinny, so it will get as much sunlight as possible, as well as avoid "drowning." The normal rice plant of the East is some five to six feet tall. But when aided by man, the plant grows more luxuriantly, adding much more grain to the stalks; finally the slender stalks can no longer support the heavy load of grain, and they simply fall over before the grain is ripe. This is called lodging. Result: anything from partial to complete loss. Lodging is a serious problem in the high yield type of agriculture being practiced today.

Or consider what happens in multiple cropping. A type of wheat that does well during the normal growing season may not produce at all well if planted again later or earlier in the season. Thus it may be necessary to plant two different wheat crops, one that responds well during a short day, and a different one for the longer summer day (which may also be wetter or dryer, depending on the area).

In other words, what must be done is to find, or develop, seeds that will do well under the special conditions of each locality, as well as under the artificial conditions imposed by modern agriculture. One of the most important of these latter conditions is high quantities of fertilizer. Indeed, one definition of a high yielding crop is one that responds well to large doses of fertilizer.

The great breakthrough in rice and wheat has come about through the ability of plant breeders to change the shape and size of these plants so that they do not lodge under intensive farming methods.

A new high-yielding variety of rice.

Before we can go into the question of how plant breeders overcame this problem and others, it is important to understand that there is not just one type of rice or wheat or corn. There are dozens, perhaps hundreds or even thousands, of different varieties. Some grow well in one type of climate and soil and some in another. Even in the same growing area, one may yield poorly but be highly resistant to local pests. The end result may be a higher yield from the second type than the first.

Rice and other grains, like humans, reproduce sexually. This means there are a male and female, and it means that the offspring will carry characteristics of both parent plants. Where a single type of plant grows in an area the offspring will be virtually identical to its parents. It was found long ago, however, that plants and animals can be "crossed." A male of one type can be cross-pollinated (e.g., by "dusting" a selected plant with its pollen) or mated with the female of another. The result will be a plant or animal with, hopefully, a combination of the desirable characteristics of both parents.

Plant scientists who traveled or were otherwise able to obtain plants or seeds from different areas tried crossing different varieties of plants. By keeping track of what plants were crossed and the results obtained, they were able to develop a multitude of different types of plants, and to reproduce the ones having the more desirable characteristics.

But even among a single species of a natural plant in a given location, there will be some differences. Sexual reproduction is useful in that it constantly brings about new combinations of the various characteristics. These may be useful in the face of changing conditions.

When plant scientists do the crossing, they can seek out certain characteristics and breed them into the plants, thus creating new varieties. The Japanese first came up with a *dwarf* variety of wheat—it was short, strong, stiff-strawed.

79

Although we shall have more to say about the Green Revolution in the next chapter, this could be called the beginning. For the short varieties have by and large taken over and have proved their worth by the results.

Hybrids

If the two parent stocks are different enough, the resulting offspring—if there is one—is called a hybrid.

A rather surprising, and very useful, attribute of hybrids is that they are often more vigorous, stronger, or, in plants, more luxuriant than their parents. Probably the best-known example is that of the mule, a cross between a female horse and a male donkey. The mule has acquired a poor reputation that is generally undeserved. Though smaller than the horse, it has much the same speed and strength of that animal, along with the sure-footedness, endurance, and patience (lack of excitability) of the donkey. The wranglers who take tourists on mule trips down the steep trails into the Grand Canyon would never dream of using a horse for the job.

The advantages of hybridization in plants is beautifully demonstrated by hybrid corn which first became a commercial reality in the 1930's. At that time yields were in the area of 25 to 30 bushels per acre. As a result of widespread use of hybrids since then the average yield, as we have seen, has risen to 80 bushels per acre, and for some farmers as high as 150.

But because characteristics of different strains of plants or animals are being brought together, the hybrid may very well be sterile, as the mule generally is. This means that the plant species cannot reproduce itself and so the seeds must continually be created anew; this is done on special farms which specialize in producing hybrid seed. Other characteristics can also be bred into hybrids; corn varieties which mature quickly (short-season varieties) have extended the northern limit in which corn can be grown by 500 miles.

Disease resistance is another possibility. Tomatoes were at one time very susceptible to certain types of wilt, a disease caused by fungus or bacteria producing wilting and withering of the plant. Most modern tomatoes are hybrids which are highly resistant to two types of wilt that were once very troublesome.

In the past 70 years or so, thousands of characteristics in hundreds of plant species have been catalogued. This "bank" of knowledge forms a foundation for much of modern plant breeding.

It would be nice if the plant breeder could, after breeding a highly successful plant, sit back and bask in this success. There are two major reasons why he can't. First, as we have seen, particular strains may do well in one area, or under one type of conditions, and not in another.

Varieties of corn—genetic material for the future.

Second, and perhaps more important, conditions even in the same area change. For a quarter of a century, for example, corn hybrids containing what is technically called the *T cytoplasm* seemed to be immune to a once-troublesome disease called the *southern corn leaf blight*. The blight, caused by a fungus, had been noted fully a century ago and had caused no problem with the new hybrid. Then, with no warning, the

A good ear of corn (right) is compared with ears damaged by southern corn leaf blight.

plants no longer seemed able to ward off the organism's attacks, and the blight began to spread—slowly at first but later with frightening rapidity.

What happened? The fungus had apparently developed a mutant form, a change of some sort which enabled it to feed on the hybrid corn plants. In 1970 ten per cent of the corn crop was affected.

Other types of seed are more resistant to the corn blight; they haven't been used much because they don't yield as well but the farmers would now be happy to put up with that. Unfortunately, because the vast majority of the corn that has been planted in the United States is of the T type, there is very little of the resistant seed available. It must be produced. Farmers are holding their breath to see what happens. There are fungicides, but these won't work once the fungus has established itself. On the other hand, spraying the entire acreage "just in case" is extremely expensive.

Hopefully a new strain, or strains, can be developed which will again be resistant to wilt and be as high-yielding and easy to grow as the T type. To help accomplish this, and to avoid similar problems with other major crops, plant scientists have set up seed banks containing tens of thousands of different strains. Collectors visit local markets all over the world, buying samples of local beans at a Turkish market, rice in Indonesia, and so on. Samples · of these are then planted to see the results and to get an idea of whether it would be worth trying to cross them with other types. An international research institution in the Philippines has assembled some 10,000 varieties of rice and has begun the slow process of storing, checking, and breeding. In another such institution in Mexico, some 60,000 strains of wheat are being checked out for the same purpose.

It has been suggested that computers be put to work to help assemble a world-wide data bank. The plant breeder's work would be aided greatly if he could find out beforehand if a certain combination has been tried, and its results.

Plant breeding shows great promise of providing a more nutritious product. In South America, for instance, where some 70 per cent of the protein intake comes from corn, any improvement in the nutritional value of the corn crop would obviously be a great help. In 1963, Purdue University scientists discovered that a particular gene in corn produced twice the lysine and 60 per cent more tryptophan. These are the two essential amino acids that are most seriously lacking in ordinary corn. The new corn, called *opaque-2* after the particular gene involved, also contains 25 per cent more protein overall. Thus far, the resulting hybrids still have a softer skin than normal, making them more easily attacked by insects and less amenable to machine harvesting. Also, they do not yield as well as the T type. A newer development, floury-2, seems to have overcome at least the yield problem.

The significance of the new corn strains is perhaps best illustrated by the following occurrence. A group of 150 South American children who were seriously ill with kwashiorkor were fed a diet of opaque-2 corn meal. All recovered! Con-

A seed bank in Colombia.

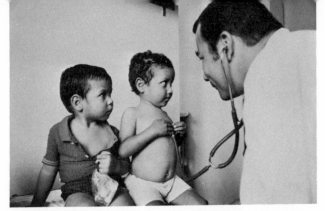

Once-malnourished children who recovered thanks to opaque-2 corn.

sidering the normal protein deficiencies of a single-vegetable diet, this is indeed remarkable. The new corns may be the beginnings of a family of high-protein grains; if so this would certainly be one of the most important developments of the century.

Crossing can take place between different crops as well as between different varieties of the same crop. A combination of wheat and rye, called triticale, has three important advantages over its "parents": a higher yield, nutritional superiority, and greater adaptability to various growing conditions. At the moment its milling qualities are still poor; this means that it is difficult to produce a satisfactory flour. But this is being worked on and will undoubtedly be licked in the near future. Other combinations are also being tried.

Another important possibility would be to somehow combine grains and legumes, so that the nitrogen fixing ability of the latter can be bred into the high yielding grain crops.

Improvements in Animals

Nor is cross-breeding restricted to plants. Although plant breeders are ahead of animal specialists, work is proceeding in this area as well. High-yielding chickens and pigs have

85

been especially successful. And milk production of cows has been increased up to 15 times; production of the average cow has been boosted from 600 to 9,000 pounds per year!

Mainly, these increases have been achieved by spreading around the qualities of few superior animals. It has long been possible to freeze semen from a prize bull and to ship it anywhere in the world. In other words a bull in Texas can be mated with an Alaskan cow. It takes only a phone call and the mailing of a small package.

It may soon be possible to do something similar with fertilized eggs. The eggs, containing topnotch crosses from prize animals, could be shipped anywhere and perhaps implanted in any cow in good health. She would then carry the egg and nurture it till birth. The poorest farmer could then obtain high grade material to work with.

In this fashion a superior cow could give birth to as many as a hundred times more calves than the ten or so she now produces.

One of the problems in animal breeding is knowing what you've got. It is not always easy to tell just how much meat there is on the back of an animal, and one doesn't cut open a multi-thousand dollar bull to see. In other words some calves will put on lean meat while others will grow fat on the same ration. The animal with the better meat can be worth $50 more. A new process using high-frequency sound waves has been developed which can probe the thickness of the fat cover and measure the size of particular meat areas. Another method uses atomic energy. The most desirable animals are then used as breeding stock rather than being slaughtered for meat.

But, as with plants, breeding can be done for reasons other than increased quantity. For instance, it may be possible to select or create cattle that are highly efficient in their use of nitrogen. One way would be for them to secrete urea into the rumen (first stomach) from the bloodstream instead of excreting it in the urine. This would save the farmer the necessity of adding high-protein foods or urea to their diet. It is said that Cuba is making strides toward development of tropical cattle that can thrive on a diet consisting almost entirely of molasses. This is a high carbohydrate, low protein food that is readily available on the island whose main crop is sugar cane.

Such a development, along with an interesting report from New Guinea, may have important implications for man. It seems that many New Guinea natives are healthier than they should be. Their diet consists largely of sweet potatoes, which are low in high-quality protein. It may therefore be possible that they have in some way developed bacteria, probably in their stomachs, that permit nitrogen fixation to be carried on. Perhaps we can select bacterial strains that can do this in anyone's stomach; or perhaps a change can be made in the human digestive system which will make this more practicable.

From the Inside Out

In these days of rapid genetic progress* the idea of changing the human digestive system is not as wild as it may seem. For geneticists—scientists who work with the hereditary material of living things—are finding that a completely new approach to plant and animal breeding is already possible. The traditional approach in plants, as we have stated, is to cross two plants, then use the seed dropped by the parent plant. Other possibilities are to graft limbs or stalks from one plant onto another. As you can imagine, these processes

* See, for example, *Biology in the World of the Future,* by Hal Hellman, M. Evans and Company, 1971.

can take long periods of time to complete, especially if several crosses are necessary. Where long life-cycle crops such as apples are involved, 30 or 40 years might be needed before a new variety can be released.

Thus far, in other words, plant breeders are restricted to working with the flowering parts of plants. They are breeding from the outside in. What they would like to do, and what seems possible for the first time, is to somehow isolate the desired trait (gene*) from one plant and insert it directly into another. Or we might even be able to create a needed gene in the laboratory.

This genetic mastery would not only speed up the work of the plant breeder immeasurably but would give him enormous flexibility and much closer control over his experiments as well.

Another technique which has been helping the plant breeders is nuclear radiation. It was found, starting with Hermann J. Muller's work with x-rays in the mid-1920's, that such radiation tends to cause mutations in living things. Most mutations are harmful and cause the eventual death or sterility of the organism. Once in a while, however, the mutation may be useful to the organism or, in our case, to man. Thus, plant breeders are deliberately using radiation to cause mutations in plants (and animals). These are then grown to adulthood and checked for useful features. A high-protein wheat strain and dozens of other useful and potentially useful characteristics have been created in this way.

Techniques like these may someday make it possible to redesign plants from the roots up. Perhaps we will see tailor-made vegetables which combine all the characteristics of high yield, high nutritive value, excellent taste and

* Each gene carries instructions for carrying out a particular function in the cell, or for the manufacture of one of its constituents.

88

texture, extreme resistance to disease and pests, and a high degree of uniformity (for mechanical harvesting). Good cooks are often fond of mushrooms. How about high-protein mushrooms? Perhaps we will even see square-sided fruits and vegetables to promote ease of packaging.

Even more to the point, enormous quantities of green plant life grow in humid tropical areas the year 'round, yet most of it is not usable. Or what is, is of the high-carbohydrate, low-protein type. How about creating plants which increase either the protein level or perhaps even the ratio of edible to inedible parts?

Professor Sherret S. Chase, a plant geneticist, believes that "the genetic engineering of the major food grains is one of the most exciting things man is doing today."

Lester R. Brown, who had much to do with the creation of the Green Revolution, feels that the new seeds "may be to the agricultural revolution in the poor countries what the steam engine was to the Industrial Revolution in Europe."

7

The Green Revolution

IN HIS EARLY DAYS MAN, like the African Bushman of today, was engaged in a never-ending quest for food. Some think he ate only meat, but actually berries, fruits, nuts, and vegetables formed most of his diet.

Modern findings have shown that he was not really as primitive or backward as we have been led to think. He did practice some ceremonies, he created some extraordinarily beautiful art work, and he produced some excellent handcrafts. Nevertheless he was by and large a savage; tied to his quest for food, he had relatively little time to develop further or to spend on improving his culture or his mind.

This was his status some ten or eleven thousand years ago—and it had been his status for tens of thousands, perhaps even hundred of thousands, of years before that. The invention of agriculture—the controlled production of food on the land—changed this picture. It increased the amount of food that could be produced by a single person or family. The improvement was such that one man could reliably produce enough food for a number of other persons. This meant that these others were then freed to do something else. The ancient Greek philosopher Aristotle said it well: "When

90

nearly all the necessities of life were supplied, men turned to philosophy as a leisure time occupation." In other words, freed from constant preoccupation with food, man could begin to develop himself as a social and intellectual animal.

Today, of course, eating is as much a social occasion as it is a way of getting nutrients into our bodies. Even the word agriculture has within it the word culture, which has very important social and intellectual meanings.

We now stand at the portals of a second agricultural revolution, one that has, in its way, equally important ramifications. Without the first agricultural revolution, man might simply have stayed where he was. Today, without huge increases in food production half of humanity may not only remain where it is, it could conceivably regress to the level of the early savages.

Hungry people react in various ways. To put it very simply: if a man is hungry and knows there is no food around, he may be unhappy but he will probably not be angry. He is more likely to be passive and dull. Anger does no good in this situation and there is no one to be angry with.

If there is food around, or the promise or possibility of food, he is more likely to become angry and may even lash out at those who are trying to help him. For example, two American volunteer workers spent several years in a South American country, helping to distribute food packages from the United States. It sometimes happened that not enough food arrived. Several times the Americans were accused of having stolen the "missing" food!

The peoples in the LDCs are, through radio, television, movies, and other mass communications media, becoming aware of the kind of lives being lived in the DCs. The chances are that they will no longer be willing to put up with the kind of conditions under which they have lived. If they become desperate enough, and angry enough . . .

But this must not be allowed to happen. And fortunately the second agricultural revolution, the Green Revolution, has given indications that all of mankind can be fed—if not sumptuously, at least adequately. Here's how it came about.

The Beginnings

Few technological developments can really be said to have a beginning. In almost every case, the "beginning" can be traced back to, or depends on, an earlier development. This is true of the Green Revolution as well. Hermann J. Muller, Luther Burbank, Gregor Mendel, plus hundreds of virtually unknown breeders who have worked on bringing forth improved breeds of animals and plants (such as the hybrid corn mentioned in the previous chapter) have laid the foundations.

Yet if a story is to be told it must start somewhere. For the Green Revolution, an agricultural region near Mexico City in the year 1944 is as good a place to start as any. In the 1940's Mexico was a hungry land; much of its food was imported from the United States. "Imported" also were four young American plant scientists who were convinced that the future of the LDCs depended not on industrialization but on getting the people fed. They were invited to Mexico by the Mexican government (under the sponsorship of the Rockefeller Foundation) to test their ideas. Stated simply, their objective was to get science to do for the LDCs what it had done for the DCs in the way of food production. For, as Lester R. Brown has put it, they "believed that the future of these countries would be decided in the countryside."

This has turned out to be a remarkably wise and important observation. Equally important is the fact that they were willing to act on their belief.

Twenty-six years later one of those four men, Dr. Norman

E. Borlaug, was still in Mexico. Using many of the principles discussed in the last chapter, he was still working on carrying out that original objective. In recognition of the original vision, and particularly the dedicated work of Dr. Borlaug, Sweden awarded him the 1970 Nobel Peace Prize, one of the most respected prizes in the world.

But things have changed considerably since those early days. For Dr. Borlaug now has a large and important research organization behind him, the International Maize and Wheat Improvement Center (CIMMYT). Established in 1966 by the Rockefeller and Ford Foundations in cooperation with the Mexican government, its activities range from basic training courses for farmers and government aides to complicated research projects for highly trained scientists. Technicians from other countries, almost 200 of them from 29 countries, have been trained as well.

Although this training has been extremely important—many of the top technical people in the LDCs have come out of a tough, seven-month crash course—it is the research activities that have been at the heart of the revolution. The first break came in 1946 when a scientist assigned to the American Army of Occupation in Japan noticed some strange-looking dwarf wheat. He brought some back to the United States where the seeds were used to produce a semi-dwarf wheat which yielded very well.

Dr. Borlaug heard about the Japanese and the American varieties and tried them both out. He got exactly nothing. All of it was lost to rust, a plant disease causing a reddish discoloration. But, with the good miserly instincts of the scientist, he had saved a few kernels of each of the varieties and he tried them out at another test plot on the west coast of Mexico, just south of the United States border. They grew there and, says Dr. Borlaug, "we crossed them with everything we had."

By working with the two sites, which differed in day

length and temperature, as well as a number of other factors, he was able to produce a dwarf variety that was well adapted to a wide variety of growing conditions. This was a major advance. Before this, most grain crops grew well only under conditions similar to those in which they first appeared or were bred.

The first major test of that newly developed wheat reads like a fiction thriller: in 1965 India and Pakistan, both in serious nutritional trouble, heard about the new wheat and ordered 200 and 250 tons of seed, respectively. Although it was already late in the growing season, the last ship that could get to India in time was already in the harbor at Los Angeles. Dr. Borlaug managed to round up the seed, and the trucks were on their way—only to be held up for two days by the Watts riots. When they finally got through there was another delay because of a mistake in the shipping papers! When Dr. Borlaug straightened that out, all seemed well until war broke out between India and Pakistan. So the seed had to be put onto separate ships at Singapore.

As a result of all the delays some of the seed had been damaged and only about half of it grew when it was finally planted. But even so, the results were far better than the Indians had ever seen. Out of this came an order for 18,000 tons of new Mexican seed—the largest single order ever placed up to that time.

The results were up to ten times the previous harvests, and the Green Revolution was under way. Many other countries, such as West Pakistan, Turkey, Afghanistan, Iran, and Tunisia, now are also involved.

There were initially, and there remain, questions about whether farmers will try something new, such as the new seed. Obviously they cannot be forced to do so, and farmers are traditionally very conservative. Even when they see high

yields they may attribute it to good weather, good luck
or some other factor. And indeed it is sometimes hard to
predict just what the best way would be to introduce a new
seed. In the early days of the wheat experiment, the farmers
would not buy the seed. Nor would they use it even when
it was given away. But, reports Dr. Pirie, "When not very
adequately fenced demonstration plots were set up, enough
seed got *stolen* at the end of the year to open the way for
general improvement."

Other Institutes

But there are many areas of the world where wheat and
corn are not considered desirable foods. It would have been
unrealistic and unreasonable to expect all LDCs to turn to
wheat and corn farming just because high yields were
obtainable. This is especially true in Asia where over 90
per cent of the world rice crop is produced and consumed.
Fortunately, the CIMMYT approach was recognized as a
good one fairly early, and three other institutes have therefore been created along similar lines.

The first of these to be put into operation was the International Rice Research Institute (IRRI), which began operating
in 1962. Funded jointly by the Rockefeller and Ford Foundations, it is located near the College of Agriculture of the
University of the Philippines. Again, the results have been
remarkable. In 1968, for example, the Philippines had a surplus of rice for export for the first time in 50 years!

Richard Bradfield, associated with both the Rockefeller
Foundation and the IRRI, writes:

One of the most significant results of these early trials [on
new strains of rice] was their effect upon the scientists, gov-

Rice breeders at the International Rice Research Institute.

ernment officials, and farmers of the region. They saw, many of them for the first time, that yields of rice three to four times as large as their average yields could be produced in their own state and on their farms. They saw new visions, developed new enthusiasms, and acquired new hopes.

The spread of the new techniques and seeds has been nothing short of spectacular. Between 1965 and 1969, land planted in the new types of wheat and rice mushroomed from 200 acres in 1965 to 34 million in 1969.

The tropics have yet a different set of problems (land, water, etc.) about which we have already spoken. To handle these problems, two new institutes have been, or are being, set up. One is the International Institute of Tropical Agriculture in western Nigeria, where the objective is to increase the output and quality of such crops as corn, cow-peas, soybeans, peanuts, and cassava.

Nigeria was chosen as the site for the institute because the population growth rate (about 2½ per cent) threatens to cancel out hoped-for improvements in the current yearly income of about $75 per person. Many of the inhabitants suffer from hunger and malnutrition, and protein is in partic-ularly short supply. And, finally, the disease and insect problem is typical of that found in other hot damp areas.

Workers from the International Institute of Tropical Agriculture weighing cassava.

The fourth institute, the International Center for Tropical Agriculture, will concentrate on the potential for raising livestock in the tropics, although it will do some work on crops, especially high-lysine corn, as well. This center is located in Palmira, Colombia. Because protein is in such short supply in many of the tropical areas, it is hoped that by finding, raising, and/or breeding animals which will do well in the tropics the protein problem can be eased. In many areas where agriculture is not practicable, it might be possible to find or breed animals that will provide good meat protein and that will put the natural year-round growth to good use.

Although these institutes have done, and continue to do, fine and useful work, they can not and must not be thought of as the final answer to the food problem. First of all, there are too few of them. The food problems of the world are many and varied. Agricultural and nutrition experts hope to see more such institutes set up in various other places to serve, for example, desert and arctic regions.

Second, these large institutes must take a "broad-brush" approach. They cannot be concerned with the individual problems of local areas. This is the function of smaller regional and national agricultural centers such as our land grant colleges and agricultural experiment stations.

Third, they cannot be expected to train technical men in the numbers that are necessary. About all that can be hoped for is that they will be able to "train the trainers."

On the other hand, the independent nature of these institutes (they are funded mainly by the Rockefeller and Ford Foundations, along with a few other, smaller foundations and contributions from various countries) gives them an advantage that they have so far been able to exploit. They can operate in areas even where the risk of failure is high. This is enormously useful. They don't have to show results, which means they can take chances. The approach can be as imaginative as the leaders please, and often it is the long shot that pays off most handsomely. Funding is on a long term basis, so planning can also be long-range, without fear that a change in the country's administration will cut off or reduce funding, as is happening in many areas of our own country today.

The results have not, of course, been 100 per cent successful. In Argentina, for instance, hybrid corn received a bad name because it was not properly introduced into the country's agricultural system. In Tanganyika, a scheme for producing groundnuts (peanuts) failed miserably. But these have been relatively rare.

There are more serious problems. In many areas it is only the better-off farmers who are benefiting, since they can afford the new seed, the fertilizer, the irrigation, and all the other higher expenses involved in the new approach to food growing. In what is probably the major irony of the Green Revolution, the Mexican dwarf wheats have spread rapidly and successfully throughout much of Asia and parts of North Africa. But they have had little impact in Latin America outside Mexico. And even in Mexico there is a division: farmers in the southern half are not doing as well as those in the northern half.

One of the problems in Latin America and elsewhere is that many of the farmers do not own their own land; they work land that is owned by others. In some cases they receive only a portion of what they earn. If a new program succeeds, they receive only a portion of the profits; if it fails, they lose all.

In other cases, they are simply laborers. A few years ago, in December 1968, there was a clash between two groups of such farmers. One group was willing to work at the prevailing wages; the other wanted to strike until the landlords agreed to share some of the large profits they were taking in. The statement made early in the chapter about what can happen when poor people suddenly see the possibility for change is clearly shown here. So deep were the passions involved in this clash that 42 people were killed in the fighting that broke out.

To whom, in other words, should the new seed go? Should it go to the rich, who can pay for it, or to the poor who cannot? Another problem is seen in a natural law of marketing. Prices drop for items in good supply. On the coast of Turkey farmers are doubling their wheat supply. Even if prices decline, their profits will go up. But the farmer in other areas of the same region may then find himself in worse circumstances than ever.

Further, many of these countries have distribution systems that are set up for importing, rather than exporting, food. As a result, they cannot handle the sometimes unexpectedly large crop yields they find themselves producing. During the months of April and May of 1968 the schoolchildren in many villages in northern India were locked out of their schools. The reason was not teacher strikes or trouble with students. What had happened was that the buildings were the only places that could be found to store the record wheat crop that had already filled to overflowing all the available storage buildings.

One of the important aspects of a good agricultural system is planning. How much is being planted? How large a crop can we expect? Where shall we store it? How will it be distributed? How much for internal consumption as opposed to export? And so on. But one of the biggest problems is that it is almost impossible to get to the really backwoods farmer. And he, as well as the local official in his region, may have a total lack of interest in the marketing function. Certainly there is little ability along these lines. Lester Brown tells the story of an American official who tried to determine just

100

how much of India's grain crop was lost during the various stages of marketing. About the only way he could do this was to add up the percentages shown in various reports. One showed for instance that 50 per cent was lost to rodents (e.g., rats and mice); another said that 15 per cent was lost to cows, birds, and monkeys; and so on. When he totaled up the figures in all the reports, it became clear that the total amount of grain lost just during the marketing process was 105 per cent of the crop!

Nevertheless, it is fair to say that the major problems, so far, of the Green Revolution are problems of success. They are problems that are arising because of high crop yields.

There are problems in distribution; but it is up to the governments involved to find some way to distribute the benefits gained. There are problems in transportation. Poor farmers, for instance, don't need roads. They can carry their produce to market on a donkey or even on their own backs.

High yielding areas will need new roads, new processing facilities, new storage facilities.

Having seen what is happening in the LDC of today, let's now try to imagine what the farmer of the future will be doing.

8

The Farm of the Future

IRRIGATION OF A SINGLE ACRE of farmland through a single growing season requires over a million and a half gallons of water. A single ear of corn requires 25 gallons of water for its development. For every pound of weight a steer puts on, 3,700 gallons of water are needed for him and the feed he eats.

United States agriculture, in other words, requires enormous amounts of water to perform its miracles. Estimates vary, but something like half of all the water used in this country goes into agriculture, with industry taking up most of the rest, and personal use requiring only about 6 per cent. In dry areas, agriculture may require even more; in Israel the figure is 80 per cent and in California it is 90 per cent! And the figure is rising. The state of Kansas has ten times as much land under irrigation today as it did a decade ago.

World-wide water use varies enormously, of course. It ranges from as low as 10 gallons per person per day in LDCs to as much as 1,800 in the United States. Therefore, predicted water use cannot be figured on the basis of expanding population alone. As undeveloped countries begin to develop, their rates of water usage will leap. And although the new varieties

By swinging in a wide circle this apparatus irrigates
a large land area.

of food crops are more efficient in their use of water they do
require more overall due to the greatly increased yields.
Indeed the new crops can only do well if they get a good
supply of water. Dr. R. B. Sen, director-general of the U.N.'s
Food and Agriculture Organization, predicts that the world's
irrigated lands will double by the end of this century.

In short, water rather than land will probably be the
limiting factor in food production in years to come. In general
there are only three ways to handle the water problem.

1) Reuse what you have
2) Conserve what you have
3) Increase the supply

We consider the first method in a later chapter. Taking
the other two in order we find some interesting approaches
being investigated. A very large problem, especially in dry
areas, is evaporation. Enormous amounts of water simply

evaporate from streams, rivers, reservoirs, and lakes. One method being looked into is to cover the surfaces of still bodies such as lakes and reservoirs with some sort of chemical film that will retard evaporation. An important requirement is that the film reestablish itself after being disturbed. Floating covers are another possibility but would be extremely cumbersome.

Another great loss of water occurs when rainwater seeps down into the dry ground and is lost. It may be possible to form some kind of "crust" on higher areas with chemicals that bind the soil, so that as much of the rainfall as possible will run off into the reservoir systems.

Another approach to improving the run-off system is to cut trees in higher areas in specific patterns to control melting of snow, which provides a large amount of water in various areas. It may also be possible to cover the snow surface with various materials. Depending on need we may want to speed up or retard melting, or to reduce sublimation (the "evaporation" of water directly from the solid to the gas phase).

Irrigation

Traditional methods of irrigation utilize a spray system; again large quantities of water are lost through evaporation. Tubing with small openings is being tried—either buried or on the soil surface—to carry the water directly to the soil. It might also carry liquidized fertilizer and perhaps even pesticides through a complicated, carefully controlled distribution system. Developing corn needs different amounts of water at different times. Sensors buried along with the pipes would be able to test the soil for moisture, acidity, etc., and call for the proper water and chemicals to be supplied.

104

Applying a layer of asphalt beneath the ground's surface.

Another interesting approach which has already been tried is to put a one-eighth-inch layer of asphalt about two feet below the surface. A machine has already been designed that can do this. The layer prevents water from trickling down into deeper regions where it does not help the crops. On Taiwan it was tried out on sandy soils in which rice did not originally do well. The result was an 11-fold increase in yield, along with the reduction of about 85 per cent in irrigation requirements.

Irrigation involves obtaining water from where it is relatively abundant and taking it to where it is needed. The All-American Canal, for example, taps the Colorado River and supplies water to the Imperial Valley in California 80 miles away. But canal losses, too, can be very high. In poorly designed and maintained canals, as much as 50 per cent of the flowing water can be lost due to seepage through the floor and walls of unlined canals, as well as through evaporation. But there is as yet no practical alternative. Buried pipelines would have to be enormous and enormously expensive. We may one day see a project called NAWAPA—the North American Water and Power Alliance—come into being. The project would take water from the great rivers of northwestern North America, pump it a total of 1,000 feet up above river level,

105

then carry it south via canals, and finally dump it into the Rocky Mountain trench; from there it would be distributed as needed to other parts of the United States.

This little project would cost upwards of $100 billion, and would take at least 20 or 30 years to complete. Aside from that there is the certainty that Canada's water needs are going to increase. Consequently they might be reluctant to share or even commit a part of this precious natural resource. So it may also be that we will not see NAWAPA come into being.

On the other hand, our own rivers pour vast quantities of fresh water daily into the oceans on all our coasts. And this is true along coasts around the world. Why not then simply stop the flow of all this fresh water into the sea? It could then be diverted into agricultural, industrial and personal uses. If we think big enough, the Sea of Japan, the Caspian, Aral, Black, Baltic, Mediterranean, and Red Seas, as well as the Gulfs of California and Mexico, can all be converted to fresh-water reservoirs.

All of this may take place, but the enormity of the engineering is enough to deter even wild-eyed politicians and engineers for the time being. There is also the danger of tampering with systems that have taken thousands or even millions of years to settle down. The vast changes that would take place could be not only detrimental but perhaps even dangerous.

All in all, it seems that there is really only one place to look for the world's burgeoning water needs—the oceans. These great bodies of water cover some 71 per cent of the earth's surface and constitute an unending source. The big problem, of course, is that the water is salty.

It is conceivable that plant geneticists will be able to develop strains of plants that will thrive on a salt-water diet. There are already some grasses that tolerate salt water, though these are inedible to humans, and also a fair amount of seaweed that is native to the sea environment. Some peoples, such as the Japanese, actually include some percentage of seaweed in their diets. It is possible that more useful, high-yielding salt-tolerant grains will be developed but it cannot be counted on.

Desalination

Fortunately a different approach is possible—desalination, taking the salt out of water. There are already hundreds of desalting plants in operation around the world. In some places desalted water is actually cheaper than transported river water. A lot depends of course on location. For regions located on or near ocean water, desalting makes sense.

But desalting requires energy, a lot of it. While all forms of chemical energy—e.g., coal, oil, natural gas—have been tried, the advent of nuclear energy really makes this approach seem practical. Although nuclear-power plants cost more than other types, the differential gets smaller as the size gets larger. This works out very well, as we shall now see.

Probably a third of the world's land is dry and unoccupied. Much of this land and, interestingly, six out of seven of the major deserts of the world are spread along the 20,000-plus miles of the world's coastlines. Many of these regions are dry because there is much sunlight and little rain.

What we have then is the remarkable combination of plenty of land, plenty of sunlight, plenty of water. Sounds almost like paradise, doesn't it?

Putting all these things together, scientists have come up with what may be the wave of the future—the nuplex, or nuclear agro-industrial complex. Basically the idea involves the building of new agricultural-industrial complexes near the sea. Large nuclear-power plants would provide the large amounts of power required. Sites would be chosen to take

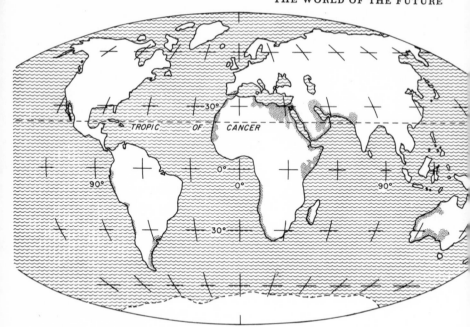

Coastal deserts which could be irrigated with desalinated water from the sea.

advantage of any natural resources in the various areas. The abundant electricity available would then be used to produce such commodities as aluminum, magnesium, chlorine, and especially fertilizers. The salts removed in the process of desalination might also provide raw materials. Location on the sea would make shipping cheap and convenient. The fertilizers, used to upgrade the land, would also be sold. The major portion of the power, however, would go into desalting the water for irrigation and other purposes.

One plan foresees a nuplex that would be based on two large nuclear reactors that would provide all power required as well as the energy to desalt a billion gallons of sea water daily. Industrial plants would produce large quantities of,

108

let's say, aluminum in various forms, phosphorus, chlorine, and ammonia. 300,000 acres of farmland as well as a city of 100,000 would round out the plan. Total cost might run about $1 billion.

One site being considered is on the northwest coast of India. Others are in Israel, Peru, and Puerto Rico.

Although the industrial portion would be an important part of the nuplex, the agricultural portion would really be basic; for not only would it feed its own population, but it is expected that the intensive farming practiced would provide food for several million others. And, finally, the nuplex would produce fertilizer as well to help feed tens of millions more.

Artist's conception of a large nuclear-powered agro-industrial complex which could feed six million persons from a scientifically managed 300,000-acre "food factory."

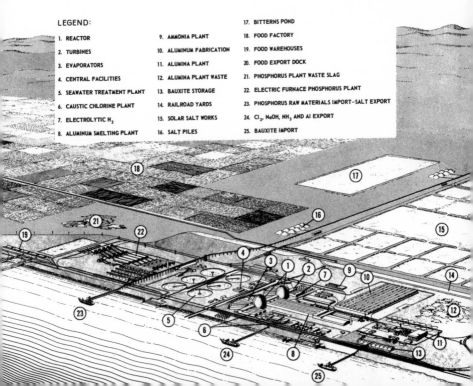

LEGEND:

1. REACTOR
2. TURBINES
3. EVAPORATORS
4. CENTRAL FACILITIES
5. SEAWATER TREATMENT PLANT
6. CAUSTIC CHLORINE PLANT
7. ELECTROLYTIC H_2
8. ALUMINUM SMELTING PLANT
9. AMMONIA PLANT
10. ALUMINUM FABRICATION
11. ALUMINA PLANT
12. ALUMINA PLANT WASTE
13. BAUXITE STORAGE
14. RAILROAD YARDS
15. SOLAR SALT WORKS
16. SALT PILES
17. BITTERNS POND
18. FOOD FACTORY
19. FOOD WAREHOUSES
20. FOOD EXPORT DOCK
21. PHOSPHORUS PLANT WASTE SLAG
22. ELECTRIC FURNACE PHOSPHORUS PLANT
23. PHOSPHORUS RAW MATERIALS IMPORT–SALT EXPORT
24. Cl_2, NaOH, NH_3 AND Al EXPORT
25. BAUXITE IMPORT

Enclosed Farming

Making the land produce at maximum efficiency is really the crux of the problem. Although there will be an adequate supply of fresh water, it will hardly be abundant. Anything that can be done to conserve water will have to be done. Thus all of the methods we mentioned earlier will be considered, along with one other that we have not yet discussed. This method is called enclosed farming, or protected cultivation, and consists of enclosing the fields in some sort of transparent "house." The idea of enclosed farming is not really new; greenhouses have been around for a long time. What is new is the notion of combining a whole round of new ideas under one roof, with the objective of producing a high yield of a wide range of crops through the most scientific methods available.

Inflation of this giant plastic "greenhouse" in Wooster, Ohio, may have a deflationary effect on the cost of enclosing vast areas.

In addition there is the development of tough, thin plastic films that can be cheaply and easily laid out and then "blown up" like balloons. No structural supports are necessary. Support for the film is provided by a constant supply of air at a slightly higher pressure than the outside. Since a number of controls will be used anyway, a constant supply of air is no problem and will cost little if anything extra.

Consider the potential controls that enclosed farming makes available:

1) Water is normally lost from both the soil (evaporation) and the plants themselves (transpiration). By keeping the surrounding air very moist (100 per cent relative humidity), water requirements are lowered by 95 to 99 per cent.

2) Temperature control (heating and/or cooling) if necessary.

3) Control of the supply of carbon dioxide. Plants need more during the hottest part of the day. This can easily be supplied. Carbon dioxide also happens to be one of the pollutants from burning of trash. This could be supplied to the plants directly in a closed cycle system.

4) Because the crops are enclosed, the likelihood of insect and other damage is reduced almost to zero, as is the need for pesticides.

5) Unwanted seeds and pollen are kept out, which means that weeds will be minimal. Again chemical needs will be minimized.

6) Without run-off of water from the fields, as in heavy rains, fertilizer use can also be very economical. Nor will some of the fertilizer run off into the region's water system as a pollutant, which is now a serious problem in some areas.

7) Air pollutants can be filtered out if desired.

As shown in the illustrations, an experimental enclosed, controlled farming installation is already in operation on the Gulf of California at Puerto Peñasco, Mexico. Staff members

Workers show tomatoes they have raised in the sand at Puerto Peñasco.

from the University of Arizona's Environmental Research Laboratory have developed this idea and have set it up in collaboration with others from the University of Sonora research station at Puerto Peñasco. At this prototype plant only 2,400 gallons of desalted water a day are pried from the sea; but already remarkable yields of lettuce, peppers, tomatoes, melons, and strawberries have been grown in what was only a short time ago a barren desert area. Construction has also begun, under the direction of the Laboratory, of a larger installation in the Arabian Peninsula sheikdom of Abu Dhabi.

Although neither of these installations is large enough to warrant using nuclear power, there seems little doubt that the experience gained in the area of controlled, enclosed farming will one day be put together with nuclear power.

In the meantime, enclosed farming is already increasing at a rate of some 10 per cent a year (from a very small base, admittedly). Of course, as much as possible of the enclosure will have to be used. Therefore not only will the plants be packed in tightly, but several layers of benches may be used. Already livestock is being kept in environmentally controlled enclosures. With livestock sunlight is not an important factor and so some interesting things can be tried. Chickens, for example, have been put on an 18-hour day, and growers have therefore been able to get one egg out of them every 18 hours rather than every 24.

Cattle and pigs are fattened up in special enclosures called feed lots. It has been found that night-lighting encourages livestock to take "midnight snacks." This helps to spread out their feed intake and they put on more weight faster.

The University of Nebraska's "Pig Mama" was originally designed to help piglets in trouble. It does this by a totally automated feeding and sanitation system and has provided much higher survival rate in the process. But it is turning out to be a sure-fire way to increase the growth rate of pigs as well.

Because so much of what is happening in both plant and animal science requires careful control and therefore protection from the elements, we may very well see multi-level farms, similar to multi-level factories, especially in areas where land is scarce due to high population. The place where this

Three ways to increase animal growth rates: night lighting for cattle fields, automatic pig-feeding bins, and a multi-storied laying cage for chickens.

is most likely to be found is inside city limits. Will we, therefore, see skyscraper farms in downtown areas? It could happen.

Weather Control and Forecasting

Another, somewhat more tenuous possibility is control of the weather. Already rainfall has been increased by seeding clouds with silver iodide. But the procedure is still far from

being consistent or reliable. There is also the problem that increasing rain in one region, if this can indeed be done reliably, may well decrease it elsewhere. The political problems would be very difficult to work out. Other techniques that have been suggested for rainmaking are the use of electricity, and superheated air fired skyward. So far nothing much has come of them. If we learn more about the weather, it may be that with an injection of the right kind of energy in the right place at the right time, we will be able to actually control it. Even the ability to just ward off severe storms, especially lightning and hail, would be highly desirable.

A reliable weather forecasting system would also be of enormous benefit to agriculture. A farmer who gets reliable forecasts of rain can save 20 per cent of his irrigation requirements over the one who simply turns on the sprinklers when the ground feels dry. It has also been estimated that a good

115

two-week forecasting system would increase yields by 5 per cent immediately.

Weather satellites have done much to help the weather forecasters. But satellites are beginning to be used for other purposes as well, such as animal surveys, and for studying such things as agricultural systems, crop-land use, irrigation systems, insect problems, even the timing of crop ripening. By using photographic techniques of various types, including infra-red, it may be possible to spot troublesome conditions in plants even before they are visible to the naked eye.

Mechanization

Although we will undoubtedly see some skyscraper farms in downtown areas, most of our food will continue to come from traditional farming areas. Aside from continued growth in use of the new seeds, the major trend here will undoubtedly be increasing use of mechanization. These two aspects of farming are actually not separate, however. For example, new types of crops will have to be developed which are better suited for mechanical harvesting, e.g., corn ears that all grow at the top (or bottom) of the plant. The ultimate objective will be "once-over" harvesting: going through the field just once to do all that is necessary for that crop.

Large machines that pick, sort, and wash fruits and vegetables are already in use on some large farms. Where multiple cropping is being practiced, perhaps the next crop can be planted as the first one is being taken in. Machines at the rear can be preparing the soil, putting in the seed and applying any needed chemicals while the unit in the front is harvesting the matured crop. Due to the importance of precise planting, prepositioned "seed tapes" have already been developed.

116

Grain combines move through a Washington State wheatfield.

Where it is not possible to get once over harvesting, other methods are possible. Experimental devices can already select lettuce and other vegetables of the right height, size, and degree of firmness for harvest. The rest are left undisturbed.

We have also seen the first commercial use of Silly Putty. A number of tree crops are harvested by means of devices that grasp the trunk and shake it. Fruits drop into waiting canvas "catchers" or are sucked up by "vacuum cleaners." The Silly Putty is used to cushion the "hand" that does the grasping so that it will not hurt the bark of the tree. One two-man crew in this way can "pick" 10 to 12 trees an hour, which is much faster than hand picking.

The next step of course is machines that run without any human intervention. Alraedy, reports the Ford Tractor Division, there is a machine that can travel along vegetable rows and pick the produce under the control of radio impulses. Such equipment can also be directed by wires buried in the ground or even by means of instructions in a computer on board the machine.

Computers

As a matter of fact International Harvester, a large manufacturer of farm machinery, has predicted that one of the most radical changes in farming over the next decade will be in the widespread adoption of, of all things, computers! In addition to directing farm machinery, they will keep accounts, monitor the progress of farm crops and livestock, figure out the best mix of feed and fertilizer on the basis of need and market price at the moment, and even figure out the best irrigation arrangement based on automatically taped weather predictions.

Indeed, on large farms computers may well be a necessity. Modern farming is very complex; the farmer must balance a large number of variables. The running expenses in a large farm—where investment may run into millions of dollars—are tremendous. Mistakes can be very costly.

Farming on a large farm and even on some smaller ones is no longer a matter of spreading around a couple of hundred pounds of some standard fertilizer or maybe even cow manure. Some people say this is too bad and sigh about the good old times. But if we are to feed our burgeoning population at the level it has become used to, there is no other way. In the past, few farmers took the trouble or had the capacity to figure out profit and loss. Many were losing money for years and didn't know it. The techniques used in the aerospace industry, called systems management, will also be required to keep large farms in operation. Already several thousand farms use computers for various purposes. New methods of use, such as tapping the capabilities of a large central computer by means of telephone lines, require only a computer terminal in the farmhouse.

The future farmer must also become familiar with a wide range of other types of scientific equipment. He may, for example, want to have one of his leaves analyzed by means of an atomic absorption apparatus. Or new types of spectrographs can show him the mineral content of his plants. If he is to make a profit he must use every tool and technique available.

Thus we will probably find that the farmer of the future will no longer be the "hayseed" we are used to seeing in the films of today. He may well be as cultured as the most urbane city man. He need no longer be cut off from the city man's culture. Improved communications—books, magazines, television—will keep him in touch with all that is happening in the world around him. Improved transportation—automobiles, trains, planes, even his own personal helicopter—will make it possible for him to visit the city as often as many suburbanites do now. And through computerization and mechanization, he will be able to manage his farm even when he is away from it.

9

Convenience Foods

THE FOODS AMERICANS eat today are not very different from those they ate back at the turn of the century. Bread and cereals, dairy foods, meats, fruits and vegetables are still the order of the day. We eat more of some things and less of others, but the basic foods we eat have not changed very much.

And yet a comparison of the typical food store of today—the supermarket—with that of the early 1900's—the old-fashioned grocery store—will show enormous differences. Mainly they involve packaging and variety. The average supermarket of today stocks some 7,000 items; most of them prepackaged under strict sanitary conditions. A visit to a grocery store of three-quarters of a century ago would have shown a far different picture. Scattered about on the floor would be large sacks of beans and rice, barrels of pickles, and boxes of crackers and dried fruits. Hanging on hooks would be hams and bacons. Then, depending on the section of the country, there might be some locally produced fresh fruits, vegetables, and perhaps meat or poultry.

Foods were preserved, if they were, by being salted, dried, or pickled. Commercial frozen foods were still 30 years in the future; even canned foods were expensive and not yet widely available. As a result, housewives had to shop at least once a day and often had to go back two or three times a day.

Although the same foods were eaten nationally, any one family had only a small sample of these foods to choose from. (It is said that vegetables were completely lacking in the diet of King Henry VIII, who ruled England in the first half of the sixteenth century.) J. B. Billard, writing in *National Geographic*, maintains that in 1900 there were less than 100 different foods readily available to the public. Today, not only do we have a far wider selection of food, but a far larger percentage of the food purchased is prepared in some way. In many cases it is ready to pop into pan or oven.

Such foods are called *convenience foods*. That most housewives prefer this convenience is shown by a very interesting statistic: The United States Department of Agriculture reports that most farm families today buy their food from the supermarket! The reasons given are that it saves work in preparation, is handier, and more sanitary.

This, in other words, is where the big change in America's food habits is taking place—in the stages between growing and eating.

As a matter of fact, even our eating habits are changing. The major difference here is that we eat far more of our meals away from home. As much as a third of our meals may be eaten or prepared away from home now—in restaurants, on trips, in the armed services, hospitals, schools, and other institutions. By 1980, one estimate suggests that the figure may rise to 80 per cent.

Nor does this mean, as some would contend, that our food now tastes worse than it did in the past, and that the situation will get even worse in the future. Foods are prepared and even preportioned in advance for airlines, for example, and are often quite good. It is less well known that many hotels and even some of the better restaurants use such foods almost exclusively.

In addition to being prepared for cooking, our food is subjected to an incredible amount of processing, for a variety of reasons. It may be coated, dyed, preserved, homogenized, pasteurized, hydrogenated, enriched, and who knows what else.

Of these processes, two are particularly interesting to us: preservation and enrichment.

Preservation

Today some 26 *billion* cans and jars of preserved foods are consumed in the United States yearly. And yet the canning process, particularly for certain foods, is not ideal. It may change the flavor, texture, color, or appearance of the food. While it has made possible the appearance of almost every type of food on our dinner tables at all times of the year and has been extremely helpful in providing a balanced diet, many who would otherwise eat some of these foods do not like them canned. The advent of new methods of preservation has helped. Frozen foods are now common. Another, newer process is freeze-drying. Here as much as five-sixths of the original weight of the food (e.g., fish) is removed, easing the shipping burden. Further, the food can be stored for fairly long periods at room temperature.

Frozen foods have had the largest impact on the distribution of fruits and vegetables. The current trend is toward more and more frozen goods; the costs of marketing fresh produce have gone so high that frozen as well as canned and dried fruits and vegetables may actually be cheaper. And certainly they keep better. Yet it is also true that many people still prefer fresh fruits and vegetables.

122

Convenience
Foods

Nor does a past trend necessarily mean a continuation of that trend. For there are counter-trends which may make a difference. Fast transportation and huge cargo planes may bring fresh foods to your table sooner and in better condition. Like cement mixers that use travel time for necessary mixing, giant "traveling factories" may process foods (grade, shell, package, freeze, etc.) on the way to market or warehouse.

New breeds of produce that stay fresh longer will help. The old-fashioned fresh corn was said to lose its flavor and vitamin content if it took more than seven minutes to get it into the pot after being picked. So some farmers would make arrangements to have the pot boiling and the horses ready to go so that the corn could be rushed from field to pot. Today new varieties of corn make this unnecessary. And it may also be possible to reduce senescence (aging) of certain fresh produce such as lettuce by special kinds of treatment.

To appreciate how this can be done, it is important to understand why food spoils. Part of the cause has to do with obvious pests such as insects, rodents, (rats and mice), and birds that may do physical damage to the food. But there is, in addition, the effect of enzymes and microorganisms.

Enzymes are substances that are important in the development of the food, such as ripening of a plant crop. There is no reason why the enzymes should stop their action just because we are ready to store the produce. If allowed to continue their activities they can cause fruits and vegetables to go past their "just-right" condition. In some cases, enzymes do not go into operation until the plant is cut or harvested. The action of the enzymes can usually be stopped by mild heating. This is one reason why canned foods are generally cooked.

It is possible that some form of chemical treatment can cut down the enzyme action. As one plant expert put it, maybe we can prevent a head of lettuce from realizing that its head has been cut off.

123

The second major factor in spoilage is microorganisms. These come in many types: molds, yeasts, and bacteria. Again heating can destroy the troublesome ones, but the heat required is much higher than that for enzymes, and this is the main reason that canned food is "different" from fresh. The advantage to frozen foods is that precooking is not necessary. The organisms that are there naturally are prevented by the cold from multiplying to an extent that they become dangerous. But the freezing and thawing may cause undesirable changes in the food.

Experiments with nuclear radiation have been tried as a means of eliminating the microorganisms, while at the same time not harming the flavor or nutritional value of the food. If this can be accomplished on a broad scale, we may be able to have a wide variety of fresh fruits and vegetables at all times of the year and in all areas of the world. To date, potatoes and wheat products have been cleared by the Food and Drug Administration for irradiation preservation.

Technicians preparing to irradiate lemons.

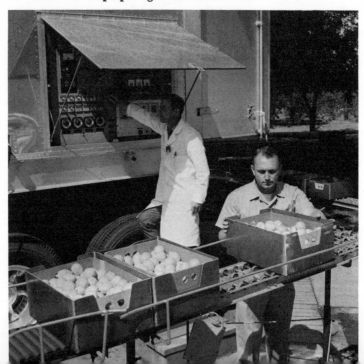

Convenience Foods

There are actually two levels of irradiation. One, a mild form, merely extends the "shelf life" somewhat. Shelf life is the length of time a food will stay in good condition after it is harvested. Some items, such as fish and strawberries, spoil quickly. Mild irradiation may increase the shelf life of strawberries, for example, from 10 to 15 days. While this may not sound like much, it may be the difference between getting to your table as a fresh fruit, and not.

Mild irradiation has been found to extend the life of such items as garlic, onions, and potatoes from two to seven months. It can also delay the ripening of fruits such as bananas and mangoes. This would spread the seasons of their availability.

Potatoes photographed 8½ months after exposure to gamma rays. The one at upper left was not irradiated while the others were exposed to varying dosages of gamma rays, and as a result remain essentially firm, showing little or no sprouting except at the lowest dosages.

The Army, on the other hand, is interested in long-term storage for obvious reasons. They are experimenting with stronger irradiation processes which may some day make it possible to store preserved foods for several years without refrigeration. Thus far, there are still changes in the food, and there is a fear that these changes may be harmful to the body. Experiments with animals are in process and should eventually tell the tale. It should be noted however, that even if experiments with bacon prove successful, this does not mean that pork and ham will automatically be cleared. So it may take a while yet before this technique becomes widespread. Sterilization (killing of germs) by microwaves is another possibility.

Enrichment

The proteins in our bodies can be thought of as a kind of chain, whose links are the various amino acids. The major difference is that a chain is made up of identical links while proteins are constructed of different amino acids. Nevertheless, the old saying, "A chain is only as strong as its weakest link," holds here as well. For if we do not get enough of one or more of the necessary amino acids, the proteins will not be constructed properly; they will truly have weak links.

As we have noted, the grains do not provide complete protein, being deficient in several of the essential amino acids. All the grains (except, obviously, for the new high-lysine corn) are deficient in lysine. The second most serious lack is that of tryptophan in corn, and threonine in wheat and rice. It is mainly to remedy these deficiencies that animal protein is important in our diets.

These lacks can, as we have noted, be made up if one is careful to include particular vegetables, such as legumes, that

126

contain these amino acids. There are obvious drawbacks to this approach, however. One is that these other vegetables may not be readily available, or "growable," in poor areas. Further, as we have indicated, the legumes do not produce the high yields of the grains. Again, new breeds may change this.

Another serious problem with the all-vegetable diet is that not many people know much about nutrition or are willing to look into it. It seems hard to believe, but it is true. Nutritionists and politicians alike were shocked to find out a few years ago that malnutrition was fairly widespread here in the United States, even among the well-off.

A major American habit is a high, and increasing, intake of snacks. One estimate puts this intake as high as forty per cent of the total diet. Most snacks, unfortunately, are high in fats and sugars, neither of which is in short supply in our diets.

Further, since so much of our food is processed, it is often difficult to find out what nutrients are contained in the food even if the shopper wants to. It is easy enough to find out how much protein or vitamin B_1 there is in an egg or a serving of chicken. But to find out about chicken pot pie or a packaged soup would require writing to the manufacturer about each item. Nor would there be any guarantee of a satisfactory answer (especially if the figures are very low, which they might very well be).

All of this may change. We are becoming more nutrition-conscious as a nation. The Food and Drug Administration is considering the idea of requiring manufacturers to list in some way the nutrition value of all foods.

Another way to meet the malnutrition problem is the enrichment of staple foods. It is already being done to some extent; vitamin D is added to milk, vitamin A to margarine, iodine to salt, and so on. Even white bread is enriched.

127

Cookies and snacks are now being enriched with vitamin B_1, B_2, niacin, and iron. Also, a fruit jam manufacturer is adding vitamins and minerals to its products.

But for various reasons that are too complicated to go into here, amino acids are rarely, if ever, added to human food. Yet this approach is widespread in animal feeds and provides good results. Since snack foods are so popular and so highly processed, they would lend themselves to the use of supplemental proteins and other nutrients. We shall see later that soft drinks with high nutritional value have already been developed and are being distributed in such areas as South America and the Far East, largely because the need for such enrichment is much greater in these areas. Reinforcing foods with nutrients might also work particularly well in such areas as the American south, especially among low-income families whose diets contain large amounts of bread and cereals.

Soybean drinks fortified to offset protein deficiency.

This macaroni, made from corn, soybeans, and wheat shown in the background, has up to eight times the protein value of regular macaroni.

Automation in the Kitchen

The high degree of preparation of convenience foods implies a great deal of standardization. It may therefore become possible, particularly in the DCs, to lighten the housewife's load not only in preparing and precooking but in other ways as well.

Unless shoppers continue to want to pinch pears and squeeze steaks, the supermarket of the future may be more of a sampling shop than a store (i.e., warehouse). Shoppers are more likely to press buttons than fill shopping carts, perhaps with the food being directly delivered to the home. Indeed, new communications technology may make it possible for any member of the family to shop directly from home, while still being able to see what he is getting. This will probably be done in connection with the new push-button telephones. He will be able to call the market, have the items he wants to see displayed on his screen, and then he will simply order by pushing the proper buttons.* The next step would be to have the items delivered and perhaps automatically shunted into the proper receiving areas in the refrigerator/freezer/pantry.

If a housewife is a working woman, as more and more women tend to be these days, it would be useful to her if she could order her dinner by setting the computer (which every home will have) before she leaves for work in the morning. The computer will figure out the right times to put up the food so that dinner will be ready when she comes home at night. And, finally, there will be a robot that will take care of the dishes and clean up the table.

There are a number of factors which make what you have just read improbable. First, the cooking part would require some form of mechanical arms to take the various packages out of storage, put them in the oven, and so on. This can become complex. Second, cooking in the future may include microwave ovens. These cook food so rapidly that setting it up in advance may simply not be worth the effort. Bacon, for instance, can be fried in 90 seconds; a hot dog in one minute; stews and soups heated in two minutes; frozen vegetables in four; and roasts and chickens in 15 (these normally take hours).

* For more information see *Communications in the World of the Future,* by Hal Hellman (New York, M. Evans and Company, 1969).

Craig Claiborne, former food edition of the *New York Times,* calls the idea of mechanical arms for delivering food from the freezer to the oven "laughable." Maybe he's right. It is said that work weeks will be getting shorter and shorter, so perhaps we'll become more interested in cooking again. Perhaps.

But you can be sure that someone, somewhere, is going to want a unit that will do all of these things. And perhaps have breakfast ready in the mornings as well. If one person has it, others will want it. That's just the way it goes. At the very least, we will surely see other changes in the packaging of food, such as plug-in packages that act as freezers, refrigerators and/or cookers; wrappings that can be cooked and eaten; and . . . well, what's your pleasure?

10

New Food Possibilities

Little Miss Muffet,
Sat on her tuffet,
Eating of curds and whey . . .

Curds and whey?

Curds and whey are, respectively, the solid and liquid portions that result when cheese is made from milk. The curds become the cheese and the whey is a liquid leftover. Clearly, curds and whey were once eaten fairly regularly. Certainly they were well enough known to be included in a children's poem.

Today while cheese is widely used, most of the whey is discarded. World-wide, some 50 to 75 billion pounds of whey are produced annually, of which ¾ is discarded. This is doubly unfortunate, for the 40 to 50 billion pounds that are discarded contain much of milk's nutrient value. Yet they are at present a nuisance, a pollutant. Most of the whey that is used goes into animal feed. Somehow we shall have to find a way to utilize whey in our foods as well.

The point is that there is much valuable nutrient-laden material which is simply discarded as waste. Yet if put to

Dr. Locke Edmondson, a research chemist in the U.S. Department of Agriculture's Agricultural Research Service, prepares to taste a sample of a new whey-cream beverage.

use it could help feed millions who are under- or mal-nourished.

The human stomach is equipped to handle an incredible variety of foodstuffs and it does. Goats' eyeballs are a treat in Iraq; Darwin mentions the use of a fungus as a staple food by the Tierra del Fuegoans; algae are harvested and eaten in Chad, Africa; Professor Pirie reports that along the upper reaches of the Amazon, the Indians add beetles to their stew—not only because of their food value, but because they "provide something crunchy to bite on." In other areas we find humans eating bird nests, snakes, calves' lips, sea urchins' sex organs, grasshoppers, and so on.

Perhaps when contamination with chemical pesticides be-comes bad enough we will just have to take our insects along with the grain or other vegetables. That might be both more tasty, and better for us, than DDT.

Actually, the utilization of whey and other now-unused foods wouldn't be as bad as it sounds at first. For much of the food that we eat is a mixture of things anyway, and often substances can be mixed in without significantly affecting taste and texture. We eat cereals, stews, breads, pancakes, and other foods into which a wide variety of substances can be mixed. A large part of the Mexican diet consists of tortillas, a thin flat bread made mainly of corn meal. It has been suggested that if the flour were prepared at a central station, rather than locally by the housewife, a better nutrient mix could be included in the flour.

Such a mixture would fall into a category usually called *formulated foods*. These are put together using carbohydrates from one source, protein from another, and perhaps fat from a third. If such food is included in your diet, that diet can still be a healthful one even if you skipped eating vegetables as many people would be happy to do.

High protein formulated foods are, of course, an obvious idea. And a product called Incaparina has been available in South America for over ten years. It was developed by a local institution (INCAP, the Institute of Nutrition for Central

Dried blue green algae harvested in the rainy season lie on straw mats in this African desert area in Chad.

America and Panama). Another formulated food is CSM (corn, soy-protein, and milk). And we have already mentioned the high-nutrient-value soft drinks. But the impact of these foods has not been as great as had been hoped. There are problems with manufacture and, particularly, distribution. (How do you get the stuff to a backwoods farmer, the one who really needs it, at a reasonable cost?) And all of this does not even take into account the difficulty of getting people to switch to new and unfamiliar foods. Incaparina, for example, has a bland taste and texture.

There are many other problems—religious, social and cultural—with the introduction of a new food. A vegetarian group in India rejected a new yeast product because it had a vague smell of meat even though yeasts are plants; a Muslim community (nondrinkers) rejected it because it reminded them of alcohol. Rice-eaters are very fussy about their rice. Many do not like the taste of the new rices or the fact that they do not cook up exactly like the rice they have become used to. Rice breeders are trying to combine the taste of the old with the high yield characteristics of the new.

The social aspects are important too. We mentioned the possibility of a centrally prepared tortilla flour. This would be good for nutrition; but the grinding of the flour by the housewife is often an important social function, as is the traditional backyard cooking of certain dishes. A group that might be willing to make changes in its food habits might not be willing to change its social habits as well.

Nor is price always a good indication of how something will sell. An experiment was run in a Chilean market; the same new food was sold at various prices in different parts of the market. The most expensive portions sold best! As a matter of fact, a new, highly nutritious food may be rejected because of what it is: a highly nutritious food intended to

135

help poor people with their diets. The problem is that every time the family members eat the food they are reminded of their position. Many in Asia will not eat bean sprouts; though they are cheap, plentiful, and nutritious, bean sprouts are associated with poverty. Similarly, foods with a lower nutritive quality are sometimes used in a poor family's diet because they are typically used in the diets of rich men. Unfortunately, the rich men will have other foods, such as meat, to supplement this less nutritious food, while the poor family will not.

In one area of the Far East it was found that a local vitamin B deficiency could have been prevented if the people had eaten their rice unmilled. The outer covering of the rice grain contained this nutrient but was ground off in the processing. But the unmilled rice took longer to cook and, mainly, tasted differently so they wouldn't eat it.

Changing Food Habits

It is tempting for well-fed people to say something like: "Hmph. If they're not willing to adapt, let them suffer." But consider. Rice is their staple food, indeed it may be their only major food, and they may have it two or three times a day. It would be a little like our having to give up all our meat and starches (potato, rice, spaghetti, and corn) for some tasteless mash, or perhaps grasshoppers and seaweed.

Also, this is not a case of obvious hunger, but malnourishment. And, similarly, it is not a temporary thing, but a permanent one. A desperately hungry man may eat grasshoppers to keep himself alive. But one who is not actually starving will be far less likely to adjust his food habits.

Nor is this restricted to the LDCs. The Germans were insulted after World War II because we shipped in corn meal to help feed them. They thought we were "rubbing it in," that we were deliberately trying to insult them. As far as they were concerned, we were giving them "chicken feed." Even hungry people have their pride. And I know personally an American couple who took a 45-day cruise to some 10 or 15 foreign countries, yet who did not eat a single meal in any one of them. They returned to the ship for every single meal. Clearly, getting them to change their eating habits would be a major undertaking.

Still the idea that it is impossible to change people's food habits has been shown many times over to be a myth. Some Americans for example, are very "daring" and will try almost anything. We will undoubtedly see a trend toward more and more different, exotic foods as the jumbo jets increase world travel and shipping of perishables. And who would have dreamed before the introduction of dry cereals that Americans would soon be starting off the day with a serving of what Professor Pirie calls "a material that resembles in texture the thermal insulation round water tanks"?

Many Eskimos have gladly taken on the white man's diet —unfortunately, for their teeth, among other things, have suffered accordingly. The white men who came to the New World learned about corn from the Indians, and it has become a major food for them as well as for others in Africa and Asia. So they too have changed their food habits.

Thus, we should not think that it will be impossible to introduce new foods. But the closer to the local food the new one is, the easier will be its introduction. Where the peoples are accustomed to mixtures such as cereals, curries, sausages, and meat pies, the introduction of new, and especially formulated, foods is easier.

Also, the way a new food is introduced is important. If you can get the rich people to use it, you are immediately in business. In Peru, a high-protein bread was first marketed

137

in expensive stores. If this cannot be done, or if there are no rich people in a village, there is another approach. One researcher says he never once tried to convince the villagers to try a new food. He simply ate it himself. Soon the villagers got curious and, because it was good and nutritious, it caught on.

Nor are Americans exempt from this problem. We have seen that there are large numbers of under- and malnourished people in our own country. Not only that, but a Department of Agriculture study showed that in all parts of the country, the percentage of diets considered good *declined* in the decade 1955–65. The figures themselves are startling. In 1955, the percentage of families eating a good diet was 60; in 1965 this had gone down to 50 per cent.

One problem is that of ignorance, or a don't-care attitude. The other is that of poverty. Someone who suffers from both problems is likely to spend what money she has on a "solid, belly-filling" food like potatoes rather than a smaller quantity of a more nutritious food such as beans.

What can be done? One attack is to teach good food habits, or at least show what a good diet can do, even in poor areas. This was tried in the Republic of Haiti. It was found that there and in other, similar poor countries in the tropical areas, as many as half of the children died during the first five years of life. Yet an analysis of the food situation disclosed (in Haiti) an average shortage of 25 per cent in calories, only a 10 per cent shortage of protein, and an almost adequate intake of vitamins and minerals. This should have led to smaller people, and people low in energy, but did not explain the terrible death rate.

The problem turned out to be largely one of ignorance. A detailed examination of the foods available locally showed that by blending two of them in the proper proportions—70 per cent of any of their cereals (rice, corn or millet) and

30 per cent of the red, white, or black common bean—an adequate diet resulted! The problem was that although adults ate beans, which were locally grown, young children traditionally did not. The mothers had to be convinced. Then they had to be taught that when preparing a gruel for their youngsters, they had to add one handful of beans to every two handfuls of cereal. The mixture was then pounded into a coarse meal and cooked in the regular way.

Getting all this across was done by setting up "Mothercraft Centers" in remote Haitian villages, staffed by girls with no more than the equivalent of a high school education, plus about six weeks of special training. Mothers came with their children to learn and to become used to the new technique. The main point is that it worked, although there were some surprises. On their old diet, the first group of the 30 most malnourished children had been quiet, inactive, and not very much trouble. With the new diet the children started to become alert and frisky. At first the mothers thought the children were under some kind of curse. At the very least they began to wonder whether the additional trouble of handling frisky, inquisitive children was worth it. But of course this attitude didn't last and passed long before the first group "graduated" in about four months.

Oilseeds

Naturally in the more developed countries a different approach is necessary. One great, though as yet untapped, source of proteins lies in the oilseeds. This is a class of crops which includes soybeans, peanuts, sesame, sunflowers, coconuts, and the cotton plant! In the reverse of the curds and whey situation, the major product from oilseeds is the oil that results when the seeds are squeezed. (Try digging

FEEDING

your nail into a peanut; you will see the peanut oil, which is widely used in cooking, ooze out.) The leftover part, a semi-solid meal, is used as animal feed, fertilizer, and in glue and paper finishes. None is used for human consumption. Yet it is high in protein. With proper processing, it can contain as much as 50 per cent protein.

All in all, almost 100 million tons of oilseeds are grown world-wide. Of this perhaps 9 million tons of soybeans are used for various products in the Far East (soy sauce in Chinese foods is about the only familiar product here), and about 3½ million tons of peanuts, coconuts, and other oilseeds are also used throughout the world. But that's it. Aside from the oil, which is used mainly for cooking and other such uses, about seven-eighths of the oilseed production is not used for human consumption. A minor exception is seen in the use of cottonseed oil in some brands of margarine.

Yet Aaron M. Altschul, of the U. S. Department of Agriculture, maintains that "together, oilseeds have the potential of furnishing almost as much protein annually for man as that available from animal sources of protein. They are now a major source of protein in animal feeds . . ."

And here we see one of the major problems faced by the LDCs. The oilseeds are a cash crop, one of the few ways that LDCs can earn cash for internal development. As a result oilseeds, which can be used as an efficient way of providing protein for the home population, are being used instead in the inefficient growth of animal protein for countries that need it least. This is a difficult economic problem, for the oilseed protein is a by-product of the oil, and is easily salable. Yet soybean meal costs perhaps 10 cents a pound and is highly nutritious. A steak, for reasons given earlier, costs ten times that much.

Of course, the problem of getting people to eat oilseed protein is not a simple one. By itself the oilseed is not very

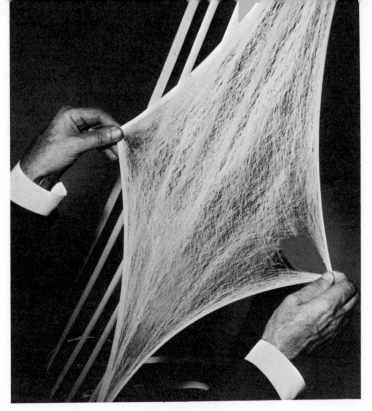

Spun soy-protein.

appetizing. One way of using the meal is in formulated foods. And this is being done to a small extent now. Another, newer process has been developed, however, which may revolutionize the entire protein picture. For it has been found possible to convert soy-protein meal into a wide variety of tasty, appetizing foods. Borrowing some standard manufacturing processes from textile industries, a few of the major food processors have been able to "spin" soy-protein into materials having the appearance and texture of meat. In one process thin fibers are formed, as nylon or rayon might be, and these are then arranged in a remarkably close copy or analog of the fibrous texture of beef, chicken, pork, bacon, and so on.

141

Perhaps most interesting is the way all of this got started. In the early 1930's (during the early days of plastics), a young Ford Motor Company scientist was given the job of trying to create plastics and synthetic fabrics from soybeans. But the development of plastics, made from other, nonplant materials, made this investigation unnecessary. Still the young scientist, Robert Boyer, remained interested in the idea. And out of it has come the above mentioned technique of spinning soy protein into meat analogs that are attractive and tasty. In truth, the process is still in an early, experimental stage, and some analogs are more successful than others. I personally have tried a smoked "turkey" luncheon meat, "pork" chunks, minced "beef," and "bacon" chiplets. All were at least passable; the last two were very good. The way they are prepared makes a great deal of difference. In some cases textured vegetable protein (or TVP®) is sold unflavored, to be used as a meat "extender."

These products are only now beginning to enter the home market, having been tested for some time in various institutions such as schools, hospitals, and prisons. The general reaction has been very favorable. In the best of the analogs, the resemblance to real meat, which is of course the most desirable form of protein found so far, is extraordinary.

There are two other important advantages of these products. One, because they are essentially a formulated food, their constitution can be carefully controlled. They can be made low in fat, high in vitamin B, or whatever one wishes. And two, they do not need refrigeration; they can be stored safely for long periods in simple plastic packages. Several firms are already gearing up for large-scale production.

The overall result is a tasty form of protein that in production is expected to be half the price of meat, and ten times more efficient (e.g., in terms of land used).

Actually it may be that this "competition" is unjust and even unnecessary. There is no real reason why TVP® should have to compete with or even imitate meat; perhaps we shall see a wholly new class of food emerge from the food technologist's bag of tricks.

It has also been found that the oilseeds can be used directly, as peanuts and coconuts are today. One interesting new product is the cottonseed itself. Cotton has long been grown for its fiber; the first records of this use go back about 5000 years. But with each 100 pounds of fiber, the cotton plant also produces 170 pounds of cottonseed. Thus far it is used only for replanting the next crop, for its oil, for livestock, and other such applications.

Other oilseeds, such as sesame, sunflower, peanuts, and coconuts, can be eaten directly or with some simple processing such as roasting. The main reason that the cottonseed has not been developed along these lines is that it contains a natural pigment called *gossypol*. Although ruminants can eat cottonseed meal, the gossypol makes the cottonseed unattractive (dark specks in the seed), indigestible, and even toxic to humans.

But because of the ready availability of all this wasted protein, and the fact that cotton is grown the world over, researchers have taken another look at the cottonseed. Two findings have emerged which give promise of making cotton at least as much a food as a fiber crop. First, a method has been found to "degossypolize" the cottonseed; more than half of the protein from the cottonseed can be obtained as a 70 per cent protein concentrate which has many possible uses in food products, e.g., in formulated foods, baked goods, etc.

In addition, however, plant scientists have developed a cotton that grows without gossypol! The Oilseed Products Research Center at Texas A & M University has produced a nut-like product from these cottonseed kernels which they call "Tamunuts." These can be eaten directly, or used in high protein soft drinks, candy, cookies, and other baked goods. Perhaps this is the way we shall make our snack habits pay off. From now until the end of the century, it is estimated that the world will produce anywhere from three-quarters to one billion tons of cottonseed. There is no reason why much of that cannot be used to produce sorely needed human protein.

But, as with all the other approaches we have mentioned, the oil seeds alone cannot do the job of providing all the extra protein that will be needed. Where else to turn?

We mentioned earlier that much of the nutrients in jungle areas are locked up in the plants. In addition, some 2½ times as much land on earth is suited for pasture (livestock feeding) as for cultivation. Thus far, the best way to convert the nutrients in pasture to human food is by use of ruminants and other animals. The problem here, as we know, is that animal efficiency is low.

But if the area cannot be easily farmed, its use for animals makes sense. What we shall probably see, therefore, is the

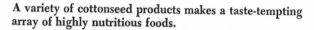

A variety of cottonseed products makes a taste-tempting array of highly nutritious foods.

use of more wild animals for human food than are used at present. How about a nice antelope, buffalo or zebra steak? Perhaps these and other wild creatures can be raised, or at least "harvested," under a process that the Ehrlichs call "organized scavenging." The herders would do the organizing and the animals would do the scavenging, meaning that they would be eating otherwise useless materials.

This would be a good combination for several reasons, not the least of which is the fact that they might not then be completely killed off, which at this time is a distinct possibly. Wild animals are also hardier than domesticated ones and are better able to take care of themselves.

We have seen, too, that Africans are among the worst fed peoples in the world. By "raising" wild animals they would be converting otherwise wasted plant protein into meat and perhaps milk. In other words, they would be putting to use a large chunk of earth that is now "wasted." (Whether we *want* to use every bit of our earth for raising food is a different question.)

As far as the DCs are concerned, beef, lamb, and pork really constitute a very narrow range of meat to choose from. Why not a wider choice? Although much of the meat from wild game is not particularly satisfying to the Western palate, animal geneticists may be able to do something about that. (Or chemical enzymes may be used to make the meat softer, and perhaps to modify the flavor as well.) A big advantage is that the animals would be collecting their own food and so would not have to be fed. If they ranged over a large enough area there would be no problem with manure piling up and thus having to be disposed of as a waste material. The Africans might then have the happy combination of a good tourist attraction that also provides food for them, as well as an export commodity to bring in more cash.

Leaf Protein

It is unlikely, however, that this approach will provide the needed calories and proteins for the fast growing population (because of the inefficient conversion of plant to animal protein). Fortunately, there is yet another approach on the horizon which might be able to put the natural abundance of tropical areas to work. Although many seed crops are hard to grow in the tropics, the fact of the matter is that virtually all the greenery that does grow is food for some animal or other. Such plants as alfalfa, water hyacinth (a major pest in warm inland waterways, including those of the southern United States), and elephant grass are actually good sources of protein; they provide good food for ruminants, manatees, dugongs, and other creatures. Humans cannot use these plants directly because of a hard-to-digest cellulose or fiber coating around the protein. But ways of extracting this protein (called *leaf protein*) are being developed. In one method, a specially designed machine mashes the leaves to a pulp. From this a juice is pressed out that contains from half to three-fourths of the leaf protein. The protein is then solidified (like cheese curd) and the end product is a cake that is tasteless and has the consistency of cheese.

Strangely, these proteins are better nutritionally than many seed proteins, and are as nutritious as some of the animal proteins. Another major advantage of using these plants is that they will grow in many areas where, because of the frequent rains, seed crops will not. The material left over after the protein is extracted can still be used as animal fodder.

If leaf protein begins to be widely used as a human food, as some scientists firmly believe it will, the lush tropical jungle will finally begin to live up to its reputation as a Garden of Eden.

146

Harvesting weeds and algae. Clark Equipment Company.

Indeed, leaf protein could turn out to be one of the most productive methods of supplying food, for the rate of growth of some plants is astounding. The record for tree growth is held by the eucalyptus, which can grow more than 20 feet a year. Bamboo, which is not a tree, may grow 100 feet in three months, though most of this growth is in the inedible bamboo stalks. Crop-type plants can grow at amazing rates too. Remember that we normally use only certain parts of plants, such as the seeds or the stalks. Only rarely, as in spinach, do we use the leaves. But a plant like the corn cockle produces green tissue at the rate of almost a quarter of a ton per acre per day.

Of course, as one would expect, leaf protein is not exactly the most appetizing dish in the world (if there is such a thing). We shall see in the next chapter, however, that something can be done about that too.

11

Future Foods

THE FAMILY HAS ASSEMBLED for the evening meal. Mrs. Jones serves—three pills each for her husband and herself and two each for the children.

Nonsense? Of course. But can you give a good reason why?

Aside from the fact that there is no enjoyment in eating a pill, we need "fuel" for our chemical engine; and we need solid materials, such as proteins, for construction work in our bodies. Because our food is mostly water, we need up to five pounds of food a day to provide us with the necessary amount of food energy and raw materials for repair and replacement.

The most concentrated form of food energy is fat; but even if we ignore our body's construction requirements we would still need a full pound of this not very palatable material. In general, the body needs at least a pound of solids a day. This would be one heck of a pill. And, of course, our digestive systems are set up to handle several pounds of food a day. We would be hungry with less.

So much for that food of the future.

No, the changes we shall see will be in the kind of food we eat, not the quantity, and in the way it is grown—or

148

made. Consider, for instance, this prediction made in a remarkable book called *The Next Hundred Years*. It was written in 1936 by an associate professor of chemical engineering, C. C. Furnas. He wrote:

> When the chemists have finished their protein pioneering, a manufacturer should be able to take sugar at 2 cents a pound, ammonia at 5, water from a river, and a bit of phosphorus and sulfur and a pinch of iron and a few other minerals and make a perfect substitute for meat protein. . . . Almost every foodstuff on anyone's menu should be synthesized cheaper than it can be grown, excepting, of course, the cheapest materials like starch and sugar.

Let us see how close we have come to being able to do this. A piece of bread, after all, is made up of nothing more than atoms of carbon, oxygen, nitrogen, and hydrogen. One problem, however, is that there are a few trillion of them, and they must be put together in a very special order and in a very special way. We are nowhere near being able to do this.

Nor does it really make sense to try.

Single-Cell Proteins

Or, maybe that's too strong a statement. It may be that such an accomplishment will come out of research into just how our food does its work. But from an economic point of view, it hardly seems worthwhile, especially since there are other ways of approaching the problem. For example, have you ever heard that a single bacterium, if allowed to multiply at will, and if given the proper nutrients, could cover the earth with its offspring in two days?

Other microorganisms, such as yeasts, algae, and fungi, can perform about equally well. The reason is that they reproduce by simply dividing in half, or giving off buds, or another simple method; and some species can repeat this little trick at half-hour intervals. Further, a microorganism, being a living thing, has a high percentage of protein; a fungus may be one third protein, and it's pretty good protein at that.

Give you an idea? Sure. Get these microorganisms to do the synthesizing for us. Of course microorganisms, and particularly bacteria, have a rather bad name, in spite of the fact that there are many useful ones. It is probably for this reason, as well as the need for a general term, that rather than being called bacterial, yeast, or microbial proteins, they have been given the general name of single-cell proteins, or SCP.

SCP has already been produced. Its main function, you will be relieved to hear, is as an animal feed (so far). Its advantages are several.

First, as mentioned, SCP can be produced quickly. See the table of doubling times for an indication of how it stacks up against other foods in this regard. You can see, for instance, that SCP grows several thousand times faster than livestock.

Bacteria	½ to 1 hour
Yeasts	1 to 2 hours
Single Cell Algae	12 hours
Crop plants	7 to 14 days
Animals	30 to 60 days

Typical Doubling Time for the Weight of Living Things.

Second, there is no dependence on the weather. Yield can be constant the year 'round.

Third, it enables land now given over to growing animal feed to be released for growing human food.

Fourth, the process is not limited to a surface, as conventional crops are. Deep tanks can be used, giving a "third dimension" to the production process.

Fifth, there is no need for pesticides or other chemicals.

Actually microorganisms have been used in various ways to change the flavor, texture, and appearance of our foods for tens of centuries. They have been used for brewing beer and making wine, for the culturing of milk-products such as cheese, yoghurt, and sour cream, in baked goods, and in many other ways.

Of the four microorganisms we mentioned earlier, only algae, which do the manufacturing job via photosynthesis, require sunlight. The other three, bacteria, yeast, and fungi, do their manufacturing work by means of fermentation. An important attribute of fermentation is that it does not require sunlight or other energy to make it "go." The microorganism changes a material, converting it from one thing to another. A yeast, for example, is allowed to "eat" a certain percentage of the sugar in grape juice and in so doing convert it to alcohol, which of course makes the juice into wine. In baked goods, the carbon dioxide produced as a by-product by the yeast causes "holes" to appear in the finished product and makes the bread or cake rise. As with humans and other animals, the microorganisms are getting their energy from the "food" they are digesting.

Now, we know that sugar is a carbohydrate and that carbohydrates can be eaten by humans. Why then is it said that SCP which we have said "feeds" on carbohydrates, won't be competing for human food?

Because it has been found that a number of these microorganisms can lunch very happily on the wide variety of petroleum products, including coal, oil, and gas!

An interesting twist is that petroleum products are members of a class of substances called *hydrocarbons*, while starches and sugars are carbohydrates. The major difference

Using wire loop, technician lifts single microorganism colony from plate for tests to determine amino acid balance in protein it produces.

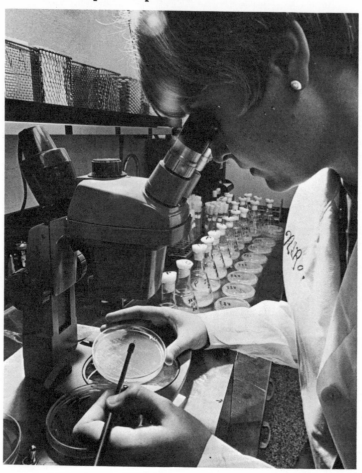

between them is that the latter contain oxygen, while the hydrocarbons do not. But both provide a ready source of carbon, which all living things including SCP need for their existence.

In other words, we now have a fast, efficient process for converting petroleum products into edible protein. Not only that, but in some cases the microbes seem to prefer parts (fractions) of the crude oil that are now considered waste.

A large number of SCP-development projects already exist in various stages, from purely experimental to a production plant yielding 16,000 tons of SCP per year. All the processes are similar, however. In a typical process, a small amount of microbe culture is put into a fermenting tank with water, air to provide oxygen, a hydrocarbon food supply, and various other nutrients. The microbes then begin to multiply rapidly; after the proper time has elapsed and they have converted all the materials they are going to, the cells are separated from the rest of the matter by some process, usually centrifuging, and then sterilized. Finally the cells are dried into a white or light powder that may be up to 70 per cent protein.

It is interesting that yields sometimes run higher than 100 per cent. That is, a greater amount of SCP results than the amount of hydrocarbon used as food. This is because some of the final product is being constructed of other materials, as for example, the oxygen blown through in the air. A typical yield, however, is about 85 per cent.

As we mentioned earlier, the SCP has so far been aimed mainly at the feed market, specifically the non-ruminants such as pigs and chickens. Ruminants, you recall, can utilize inexpensive foods and chemical additives such as urea, while non-ruminants cannot. Experiments with SCP have shown no distinguishable differences between pigs and poultry given supplements of SCP and those given fish, flour or soy meal.

153

Pigs raised on SCP. The British Petroleum Co., Ltd.

(These substances are used as feed supplements because they contain a higher percentage of protein than can be utilized by the livestock if used as a basic food. They are also too expensive to be used in this way.)

As you can imagine, however, the use of SCP as a human food has enormous potential. It has been estimated that only 2 per cent of the crude oil presently produced worldwide could yield 22 million tons of protein. This is roughly equal to the total annual production of animal protein, and is enough to supply one-third of the protein required for the entire world in the year 2000.

The extraordinary potential of SCP is further shown by the following calculation: a plant that could supply 10 per cent of the world's entire food needs, roughly 50 per cent of its protein needs, would require an area only one-half mile square!

Obviously this isn't going to happen. Distribution from a single plant would be a very difficult problem; SCP is still more expensive than crop proteins; and of course it is not going to be easy to get people to eat the stuff. We may call it SCP, but we are still going to hear that it is bacteria, yeast, or fungus. And it is still a tasteless, unappetizing powder.

But SCP has already been baked into cookies and cooked into cereals and soups—and eaten. The Russians are supposed to have already developed an SCP product with the texture and flavor of caviar.

Making Flavors

We spoke in the last chapter about giving texture to vegetable proteins. The same can presumably be done with SCP. It is time now to devote some attention to how the flavoring problem is taken care of. How, for example, does one give the flavor of caviar to SCP, or beef to textured vegetable protein?

Obviously, if we use actual caviar or beef we are defeating our purpose. And if we use, let's say, 50 per cent beef and 50 per cent SCP, we end up with a product that has only 50 per cent of the desired flavor. The alternative obviously is to add flavoring. Let's see just what this means.

Natural flavorings such as salt and spices have been used for thousands of years. Recently, however, chemists have been unraveling the mysteries of what constitutes a specific flavor. (The taste of a natural food may derive from a mixture of as many as 150 different substances.) Nevertheless, with their new knowledge, they have been able to make artificial flavors.

155

These may mimic natural flavors and may simply be cheaper to make artificially; or they may be completely new flavors. There are also in-between processes, in which natural flavors are processed in some way before they are added to a food.

Artificial flavors are used in the TVP we discussed in the last chapter, and they are being used more and more widely in formulated foods. For example, a United Nations agency developed a food supplement known as PKFM, which contains 20 per cent protein, 15 per cent sugar, and 8 per cent

Malnourished children being fed PKFM.

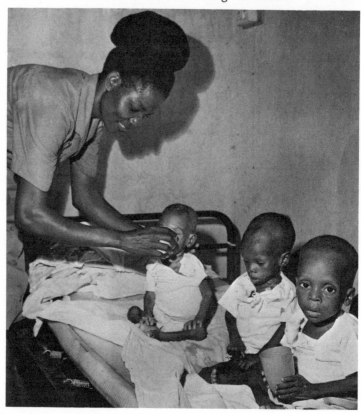

fat. To give it some taste, a specifically formulated and blended vanilla flavor was developed (by a company called International Flavors and Fragrances), and two tons of it were produced to add to the PKFM. Through July of 1970, PKFM had been given to more than half a million children to help their nutritional condition.

In 1968, flavorists at IFF introduced new onion, garlic and mushroom flavors. And in a recent annual report, the firm reported that dried blue green algae harvested in the rainy season has long been used for food in an African desert area in Chad. IFF flavorists hope to make the taste and color of this high-protein natural food acceptable for use in the many desert areas of the world where it might be produced more cheaply. And of course artificial flavors will be used in SCP when it goes on the market for humans. (I have no doubt that it will. Do you?)

Food flavors are part of a class of substances called *food additives*. These are added to foods either for nutritional purposes, as with vitamins and minerals, or for what might be called functional reasons. In this use they might be added as a way to hasten some step in the processing of the food, to protect the food from decay, to improve its appearance, or most recently simply to make something with no, or poor, taste more palatable, as in the PKFM mentioned above.

In recent years the use of food additives in the United States has increased by some 50 per cent, largely due to increased intake of convenience, formulated, and otherwise prepared foods. Each of us now takes in an average of 3 pounds of food additives per year.

Not everyone, it should be noted, is happy about this. Some believe that some of these additives may be harmful. One report maintains that the U.S. food industry uses some 2,500 additives, of which only half have actually been tested for safety. And indeed some additives that had been believed

A highly magnified photograph of microcapsules containing a flavor compound.

safe and were widely used were later found to be harmful and were withdrawn from the market. This is still a wide-open question. About all that can be said for sure is that what some people claim, namely that all chemicals are bad for you, is not so. Salt is a chemical and so are vitamins and minerals. On the other hand, *too much* salt *is* bad for you.

James S. Turner, writing in *The Chemical Feast*, maintains that coloring additives, preservatives, seasonings, and tenderizers camouflage the rapid increase of fat content in frankfurters (in 1969 it averaged about one-third by weight), the decrease in meat protein, and the substandard quality of the meat.

The buyer will simply have to continue to be careful of what he buys. Hopefully, new labeling laws will require that sufficient information be given the buyer so that he will be able to determine what he is buying.

We would also hope that improved methods of analysis will give a clearer picture of what is harmful and what is not. For clearly many additives are useful and harmless. The important thing is to be sure that only the safe ones are used.

We may also see something else of interest on our labels in the future. A chemical called PTC is not tasted at all by some, while it is found to be extremely bitter by others. Fred L. Whipple, writing in *The Scientist Speculates*, suggests that we may be able to find similar classes of taste in other areas. If so, we could label cans and other packaged foods in such a way that one would know automatically when a food, or perhaps a way of preparing a dish, will not be to our taste. This, of course, will be effective only in cases of true chemical incompatibility. In many cases we don't like certain foods because of unfamiliarity, or for cultural or other such reasons.

Manufacturing Food

Let's return now to the question of true synthesis: the use of chemistry to put complex molecules together to manufacture food. Experiments with duplicating the photosynthetic process indicate that at least this process can be accomplished outside the green plant cell. Initially, experimentation is being aimed at manipulating the process to produce nutritious food from presently unusable plants or to increase the protein content.

We know that photosynthesis is an inefficient process. Also intensive cropping requires large amounts of synthetic nitrates; the power required to make the food directly (artificially) may not be too much more. And, finally, great advances have been made in the laboratory synthesis of amino acids and simple proteins. Perhaps, as Furnas predicted, we may yet have great food factories that turn out some better tasting, more attractive, more nutritious food than we can even imagine now.

There is very little likelihood that factory production of food will displace farm production altogether. This is particularly true of sugar and grain production. These crops are still quite cheap and relatively plentiful. Professor Pirie points out that "the development of this aspect of food technology [synthesis] will be slow because the countries that are best able to undertake it are not those that suffer at present from a food shortage."

One slightly more feasible method of producing food artificially is a technique called *tissue culture*. It has been found that living tissue can be grown even though separated from the rest of the living thing it originally came from. Skin or heart tissue, for instance, can be kept alive and growing if it is fed the proper nutrients and if the wastes it produces are flushed away. Thus we may find enormous vats in which ham or sirloin or veal are grown. There would be major advantages: no fat or bones to dispose of; no problems with insects or disease; and no waste of grain for production of such wasteful animal parts as hoofs, horns, and hair.

A final hint from history. At the turn of the century, all our clothing and other fibers came from plants and animals. If you had said then that by 1970, half the fiber in the United States would be produced artificially, you would have been thought out of your mind. The same thing holds for non-food additives to livestock feed.

160

Today half the fibers used are synthetics, and substances such as SCP and urea are widely added to livestock feed.

Will half our food be synthetic 70 years from now?

Stranger things have happened. Clearly a lot will depend on just how desperate the need for food is at the time.

12

Food from the Sea

THE OCEANS COVER some 71 per cent of the earth's surface. There is, therefore, more than twice as much ocean as land surface. Further, the average depth of the oceans is about 2½ *miles*. In other words, there is an enormous volume of water for marine life to develop in. This should provide enormous amounts of food for man. Yet the total ocean catch is only about 60 million tons; this provides only some 3 per cent of the world's protein and 10 per cent of the animal protein.

Why? Is the problem simply that we haven't been able to get to all of this food?

Strangely enough, the answer to that question is no. Dr. J. H. Ryther, of the Woods Hole Oceanographic Institute in Massachusetts, maintains that 90 per cent of the world's oceans are a "biological desert."

To understand why this is so, we must look at the so-called marine food chain. By this we mean a group of organisms, each member of which is eaten by the next member. As on land, the first link in the chain is forged by the process of photosynthesis and is also fueled by the sun. This is important because it tells us that basic production of marine food is

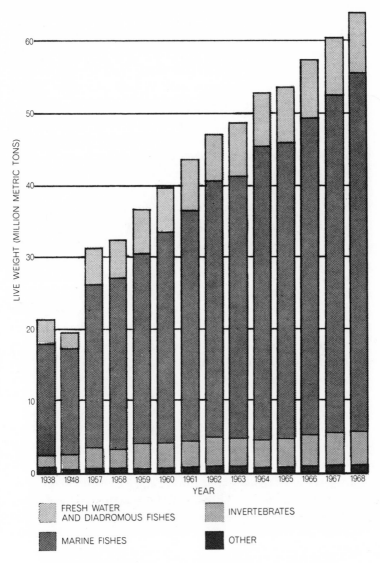

LIVE WEIGHT (MILLION METRIC TONS)

YEAR

FRESH WATER
AND DIADROMOUS FISHES

MARINE FISHES

INVERTEBRATES

OTHER

World fish catch has more than tripled in the three
decades since 1938. The largest part consists of marine
fishes. Humans consume only half of the catch; the
rest becomes livestock feed.

limited to the upper layers of the sea, beyond which the sun does not penetrate.

Further, the sea plants that carry out the process of photosynthesis need nutrients just as land plants do. These are less likely to be found out in mid-ocean than they are near the land masses, where rivers, rain, and wind wash or blow large amounts into the sea. Fortunately, the continental masses are surrounded by continental "shelves" which slope down gradually, sometimes for hundreds of miles, before plunging to the great depths of the ocean.

The end result is that the continental shelves, along with banks, large lakes, and shallow seas provide us with practically all our seafood. Indeed, although these areas make up only a few per cent of the total area of the ocean, and an even smaller percentage of its total volume, they produce fully 90 per cent of the world's seafood.

There is life in the deeper waters, of course, but comparatively little. Hence most of the food that does grow in the sea is relatively accessible. Dr. Ryther estimates that the total production of fish in the sea is about 240 million tons a year. Man's catch is already a fourth of that. (Much of this is used in various forms as animal feed.) He figures that the most we could take in on a steady basis (without seriously depleting the stocks—which we have already done with some species) would be about 100 million tons. This is less than twice the present catch.*

But we are talking about fish. And, like livestock on land, the larger fish lie at the end of the food chain (excluding man) and therefore constitute a small percentage of the total marine production of living things, which is something like 100 *billion* tons.

One way to increase our marine food supply, therefore, is

---

* Other estimates, it should be noted, are much higher, ranging up to 2 billion tons.

to shorten the chain, i.e., to take our food earlier in the chain. Let us look at the simplified food chain and see how this might be done.

The first link, as we know, is made up of plants. These, due to the special requirements of the ocean environment, are microscopic, one-celled plants. They float about in enormous masses and are called *phytoplankton.* Because of their need for sunlight, they are limited to the upper layers of the ocean.

They in turn are eaten by a group of slightly larger animals called *zooplankton,* which includes single-celled creatures 0.0004 to 0.02 inch in length and a wide variety of somewhat larger shelled animals called *crustaceans.*

The zooplankton in turn are eaten by small fish, and these in turn are eaten by larger fish. The small and large fish not only provide most of man's seafood but also (upon death) nitrogenous and mineral matter that is absorbed by smaller plants and animals, thereby completing the food cycle.

But when man catches a large fish, he is at the end of a long food chain, and this is the main limitation on his catch, for the higher up on the food chain you go, the less food there is. Think of a multi-level pyramid. Each level must rest on a successively larger base below it.

There are some exceptions to this simplified description. Some small and large fish, for example, are herbivorous (vegetarians). And some very large creatures, such as the baleen whales, subsist on a larger type of zooplankton called *krill.* These are shrimp-like animals half an inch to two inches long. Among the baleen whales are the blue whales, the largest creatures on earth, ranging up to 100 feet in length. Thus we see the strange spectacle of the largest animals, the blue whales, subsisting on very small ones. There is a lesson here that man is beginning to study. For what the baleen whales have done is what we suggested earlier, namely shorten the food chain.

Can man do the same? There is some talk about fishing for zooplankton, and particularly krill. For these contain a high percentage (more than 20) of food protein and have been found to have a good seafood flavor.

But there are problems. For one thing enormous amounts of water must be strained to get the plankton because it is so spread out. Perhaps a million pounds of water have to be pumped and strained to get one pound of plankton. Shelling the small creatures would also be a problem. And finally there is a slight chance of poisoning because some of them occasionally feed on poisonous algae.

As usual, however, it is dangerous to rule anything out. Methods have been found to do stranger things than this, and we may yet see great "artificial whales" or "krillships" that will scour the oceans for krill or other zooplankton.

Perhaps we can go even further back in the food chain, indeed right to the beginning, to the phytoplankton. These are found, by the way, in fresh as well as salt water. And, indeed, a common example is the slimy green growth called *algae* that is often seen in quiet water (it is often called "pond scum") and on various moist or wet surfaces.

Actually, the term algae comprises a large group of phytoplankton ranging in size from the microscopic to enormous 100-foot long seaweeds. The microscopic type sometimes forms into colonies, and this is the type pool owners must fight each summer. Great floating colonies of a large brown alga (singular) called Sargassum in the North Atlantic Ocean have given that area the name the Sargasso Sea.

In truth, marine plant life is used for food to some extent already. Some forms of seaweed are used fairly regularly by the Japanese and others. Another, rather more unusual use has been that of the smaller algal forms. The ancient Aztecs as well as the modern dwellers along Lake Chad in Africa have used them for food. Tangled filaments of a blue green algae are scooped up, dried, cooked, and made into a highly nutritious soup. Modern tests on a single-celled, fresh water alga, Chlorella, have shown that it contains useful amounts of protein, carbohydrates, and vitamin C. One researcher in California has already made cookies from Chlorella, which is handled rather like the single-cell protein we mentioned earlier in the book. That is, the same food-processing techniques being developed for bacterial and yeast SCP can be applied to making algae at least useful, perhaps even delicious. Even if algae do not become an important source of human food in the near future it is likely that they will be exploited as feed for animals.

A major advantage of algae is that they can be, and have been, grown under controlled conditions. For man at sea is still largely a hunter, and a fairly haphazard one at that. As a result some fish species are overfished and in danger of being killed off altogether, while others are underfished.

Under- and Overexploitation

Let us consider the problem of underexploitation first. New methods not only of tracking fish by sonar and other electronic methods but of attracting them—by lights, sound, chemical attractants, or electricity—will find increasing use. Netting will continue to be used, but if the attractants work, the higher concentration of fish will make it practicable to use a vacuum cleaner catching method. Great tractor-type machines will probably be used to harvest marine life on the floor—mainly shellfish like crabs, lobsters, mussels, and oysters.

The problem of overexploitation is far more serious and far more difficult to handle. Several steps will have to be taken. One is to make our fishing more scientific, more efficient. This does not always mean taking more fish; better methods of judging fish populations may tell us when to ease up before we have depleted stocks to a danger point. At present we learn this only when putting in more effort brings steadily diminishing returns. Satellites may be able to give some of this information; floating ocean buoys will probably also be used. These will add to the world's store of weather information, but will in addition keep track of the movements and size of marine populations.

There will have to be a greater understanding on the part of the various governments of the serious threat to the larger forms of sea life. A once-thriving herring industry along the east coast of Great Britain has already been wiped out by overfishing.

And there will have to be a much greater degree of co-operation between the various governments than there has been to date. The whaling industry is a good example. The large whaling countries, such as Russia, Japan, and Norway, have not been able to come to a satisfactory agreement on how to limit their individual catches; each wants to take as much as it can, and unfortunately modern whaling techniques are very efficient. The result is that several of the large species of whales, including the great blue whale, are in real danger of extinction.

As a matter of fact, the way things look now, we may end up with less food from the sea in a few decades than we get now. As the Ehrlichs put it (in *Population, Resources, Environment*), it's like chicken farmers who eat up everything while burning their henhouses to keep warm.

Greater use will have to be made of the so-called junk-fish, those that have little or no commercial value at present. (The Japanese already use some of these in fish sausages.) This will help ease the pressure on the more desirable species. Much more important in this respect is a process that converts fish into a meal or powder called *fish protein concentrate*

168

(FPC). Although the material has been widely used as a livestock supplement, until now it has not been used for humans. This will change, and pilot plants have already been built to produce the materials. There are problems, however. Not all fish can be used; some produce a fatty meal with an unpleasant flavor and smell. But various methods are being tried that may overcome this. It has been found possible to convert the oily fish meal of the alewife to a more desirable form using fermentation. Other methods are also being investigated.

There is a further question, whether to use only edible parts or the entire fish. Obviously the latter approach is far more economical, and disposal problems are minimized. But is it safe? Suppose a fish has just swallowed something poisonous. Tests so far seem to indicate that it is safe to use the whole fish, but the issue has not been decided yet. But the final product in either case is high in the essential amino acids that are lacking in vegetable protein.

Aquaculture

The problems of both under- and overexploitation can be overcome if we apply to the waters of the world the farming techniques that have proved so useful and efficient on land. The result is *aquaculture*.* This is being done to some extent already. "Bottom-dwelling" shellfish such as lobsters, mussels, clams, and oysters are being raised in bays, estuaries, and other shallow-water salt areas. There are five oyster hatcheries in Long Island Sound alone. Indeed this type of aquaculture was once larger here than it is now. F. Scott Fitzgerald once called Long Island Sound a "great wet barnyard." Oysters are making a "comeback" after having almost been wiped

* Sometimes also spelled aquiculture, and called mariculture.

Feeding baby shrimp, one phase of an experiment in shrimp aquaculture, using the waste of a nuclear generator to warm the water.

out by pollution. And some fish, such as catfish and pompano, are being raised in both natural and artificial ponds. The total yield so far of all types from aquaculture is in the area of 2 million tons, or about 4 per cent of the total marine food harvest.

This could be increased enormously. The losses, for example, of eggs and young fish to predators (other than man) are incredible. For the food chain, remember, is made up of larger living things that eat smaller ones. If man were to farm certain creatures, these losses would be reduced greatly or even eliminated.

170

Of course, fencing off large areas of the continental shelves (to keep the growing fish in and predators out) would be an extremely expensive proposition. But maybe some form of electronic fence, utilizing electricity, light, microwaves, or sound, could be developed to make the job easier and cheaper.

Nor is raising fish from the egg stage easy to do; the care and feeding of wild things is a technique that requires great skill and is not always successful.

But there are some interesting things that have already been learned. It has been found, for instance, that fish in less crowded waters will grow several times larger than they will in more crowded quarters. Clearly this is an important factor to keep in mind. Further, as we mentioned earlier, some fish, even large ones, are vegetarians. A Chinese carp is known that grows to five feet in length and gains 50 pounds in five years; equally significant is the fact that it eats 60 pounds of weeds a month. Some of our inland waters are becoming choked with weeds such as the water hyacinth. Perhaps stocking those areas with fish such as the Chinese carp is the answer to keeping them clear while at the same time providing good food to eat.

If some fish prove too difficult to raise from infancy, another interesting fish characteristic can be utilized. Some fish, such as the salmon and the steelhead trout, are born in fresh-water streams, then migrate to sea for most of their adult life. When it comes time to mate, however, they return unerringly to their place of birth! Thus it would not even be necessary to supply them with food during their major growth period. One scientist, Lauren Donaldson of the University of Washington, has developed a fast-growing rainbow trout that he is trying to cross-breed with the steelhead. The result could be a fast-growing, delicious trout that would fatten himself up and then return "home" when he is ready for the table.

In those cases which require full-time feeding there are

171

other interesting techniques being considered. Most aqua-culture, as we mentioned, takes place in shallow waters such as bays, lakes, estuaries and the like. Fortunately, these are the easiest to fence in. And since they are all fed by streams and rivers, it may be possible and desirable to "inoculate" these moving bodies of water upstream with desirable food for the fish we are interested in feeding. By the time the baby plants or animals we have put into the stream get to the feeding point they may have grown to useful size. In a similar vein, krill may never become a useful food for man, but it may very well prove useful as feed for fish being farmed.

If we would like to farm warm-water fish in colder areas, we might wish to use the waste heat from power plants to warm up the water. This is being done experimentally in such widely diverse areas as Scotland, Long Island, Florida, and the Soviet Union.

Naturally, if we are farming fish, they will require more nutrients than are naturally available. These will have to be supplied. One way is to feed them in the ways we have mentioned. Another is to copy a process that occurs naturally.

Laboratory cultured diatoms—microscopic plants— serve as food for baby shrimp. Careful control is nec- essary to bring the diatoms to maturity at the proper time.

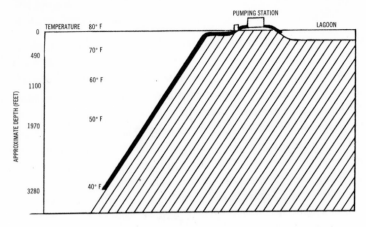

Cold, nutrient-rich water is pumped from ocean depths to accelerate production of sea food.

When nutrients enter the sea some remain in the shallow waters and are utilized by marine life. Others are carried into deeper waters and, due to lack of sunlight, are not utilized by plant life. The concentration of these nutrients (e.g., nitrogen and phosphorus compounds) then builds up. The nutrients may also be transported great distances by cold currents in the ocean depths. In some places, as along the shores of Chile and Peru, natural upwelling of these deep, cold, nutrient-laden waters takes place, and enormous concentrations of fish are produced. It is in such areas that some of the world's great fisheries are located.

What is the possibility then of piping such waters into artificially or naturally enclosed areas, such as lagoons and lakes? There are hundreds of coral atolls—rings of coral surrounding shallow bodies of salt water—in the Indian and Pacific Oceans where this might be done. Due to the nature of coral building, the outside rings of the atolls often slant down sharply into deep water, which means that the cold, nutrient-laden waters we have been discussing might be relatively close.

173

An experiment in the Virgin Islands, being run by a group from Columbia University, is even now pumping deep-sea water through a pipe and into ponds to accelerate the growth of phytoplankton. These in turn are being used to raise shell-fish. Results so far are very promising.

Perhaps we can even raise whales. Whale meat was at one time a fairly common diet item. A single large whale can provide as much meat as 20 large steers.

A number of scientists believe that aquaculture rather than fishing as we know it today will provide the bulk of man's seafood in the future. This is particularly true of southeast Asia where protein shortages combine with thousands of miles of undeveloped shorelines, bays, coastal swamps and salt marshes to make the process particularly attractive.

On the other hand, it may be that coastal salt marshes alone will make the greatest contribution of all. Professor John D. Isaacs, director of marine life research at the Scripps Institution of Oceanography, tells us that

> The higher flowering plants that inhabit the marine salt marshes are able to tolerate salt at high concentration, de-salinating seawater with the sun's energy. Perhaps the tiny molecule of DNA that commands this process is the most precious of marine-life resources for man's uses. Bred into existing crop plants, it may bring salt-water agriculture to reality and nullify the creeping scourge of salinization of agricultural soils.*

"Perhaps," adds Professor G. B. Pinchot of Johns Hopkins University, "the single most exciting challenge we have in marine farming is this opportunity to make a new start in the production of food, utilizing the ecological knowledge now available."

* *Scientific American,* September 1969, p. 162.

174

Food from
the Sea

For, as we shall see in the next chapter, obtaining the food for earth's rapidly increasing population is only half the battle. There is a distinct possibility that we are doing so at the cost of severely, and perhaps fatally, damaging this fragile bit of dust on which we are journeying through space.

13

The Quality of the Environment

WHEN A HOUSE CATCHES FIRE, the first job is to save anyone in that house; the second is to put out the fire; and the third is to see how much damage was done by the water that put it out. Sometimes the water destroys the house and its contents quite as effectively as the fire would have.

We have discussed the problem of hunger and malnutrition in the world today—this is the fire. What we must also consider is that many of the answers we have read about (the water) may be contributing to a future problem that is even more serious than the hunger and malnutrition that affect so many. For many of the solutions to the food problem are short run. That is, they produce the food increases needed; but at the same time they are causing serious damage to the air, land, and water upon which all of our lives depend.

Take the standard approach of opening up more land to agriculture. Typically a population will develop, for example, along a stream or river in a valley and all will be well. But when the valley is filled, farmers will begin to move up the sides of the valley. It is tempting to think that the only difference would be a somewhat more difficult job of farming the land. But no. Not only is farming more difficult on the hillsides but soil erosion problems become more serious. Poor run-off systems can destroy irrigation systems down below. And gullies cut into the hillsides by rainwater running down freshly cultivated lands can destroy the terrain for centuries to come. In one area of West Pakistan, gullies cut in hillsides became so large they turned into a minor tourist attraction.

It may take thousands of years for an inch of topsoil to form. Loss of this topsoil by erosion, or even overgrazing, can turn a potentially productive area into a desert. Irrigation without good drainage can cause the salts and other minerals contained in the water to make the land too salty or "alkaline" for good farming. Increased irrigation can lower water tables elsewhere, thus allowing salt water to seep into the soil from a nearby ocean. This is already happening on Long Island.

Increased, and careless, use of pesticides and fertilizers can ruin good farmland and pollute streams as well. Often, a pollutant is nothing but a useful material in the wrong place. A pesticide in the mouth of a harmful insect is a good thing; in the gullet of a bird it is a bad thing.

The same is true of fertilizers. And it is even true of topsoil! On the land, it is fine. But careless cultivation can cause run-off into streams, polluting them seriously. Two professors at Penn State, L. W. Saperstein and T. V. Falkie, point out that "our agricultural methods are not perfect . . . indeed, the entire agricultural process can be viewed as a devastating blow to the natural ecological cycle."

Another very serious problem is the natural waste produced by livestock farming. A single cow produces as much organic waste as 16 people. Thus a large feed lot with 10,000 cows will produce as much manure as a city of 160,000 people. One chicken farm on the West Coast must dispose of 120 *tons* of chicken manure a day. The cost of doing so has become a substantial part of the total cost of operation. The *New York Times* reports that agricultural waste is

> the largest single source of unwanted material in the country, accounting for two thirds of about 3.5 billion tons of solid waste produced every year. . . One and a half million tons of this is the manure from farm animals such as cows and chickens. About 550 million tons is leftover waste from the marketable portions of farm crops.°

Clearly some of this could be used as fertilizer. The problem is that in order to make livestock raising more efficient and productive, the animals have had to be penned closer together. As a result, very small areas produce enormous amounts of manure. And, unfortunately, farmers have found it cheaper and more expeditious to buy artificial fertilizer than to haul and distribute and use the animal wastes. In India, by way of contrast, manure is used not only as fertilizer but as plaster in building and, most important, as fuel in cooking. Indeed, cow dung is India's main cooking fuel.

It is not likely that we shall be using cow dung as plaster or fuel—at least not in the near future. What will happen in a century or two if we continue to use fossil fuels (coal, oil, and gas) at our present rate is harder to predict.

We are slowly realizing, however, that ways must be found to utilize these enormous amounts of agricultural wastes—in other words, to *recycle* them. The same holds true of course for the wastes generated by people and industry. After all, the materials of which we, and all living things, are composed exist in large but not infinite quantities. They must be used over and over. We can no longer afford to simply throw out the by-products of our production. This kind of behavior may seem to make sense to the chairman of the board of a large corporation, but it certainly does not make

° September 15, 1970, p. 93.

ecological sense when viewed from the standpoint of the community as a whole.

This is especially true in light of the rapid increases in population that are taking place now and that, it seems, will continue. The late W. M. Myers, of the Rockefeller Foundation, warned that the increases we have seen in food production are in a sense dangerous. They seem to indicate that we can take care of larger population; but they mask the secondary effects of other, potentially more serious problems such as pollution, disease, and perhaps even the eventual total breakdown of our environment.

Consider also the problem of insect pests which cause enormous crop losses. So far, the easiest and least expensive way to control insects is by use of chemicals. Yet we may find ten or twenty years from now that we have poisoned our land and water beyond repair.

There are other ways of dealing with insects. Among the most important are biological methods, which include the use of viruses and bacteria that attack only the unwanted pests, rather than wiping out a whole chain of creatures from soil bacteria to large birds. There are even other insects and certain birds and animals that prey specifically on the unwanted pests.

It may be possible to synthesize particular chemical attractants that will cause the unwanted insects to march happily to their doom. Lights, electricity, radiation, sound, and other possible methods of attraction are being investigated.

Sterilization and release of large numbers of males of a particular species have proved very effective. Since many insects mate only once, the many sterilized males "use up" the reproductive potential of the species in that area and the numbers drop drastically. This has been very effective in controlling the pestiferous screw-worm fly in the south.

Yet another hopeful sign is the recent development of a

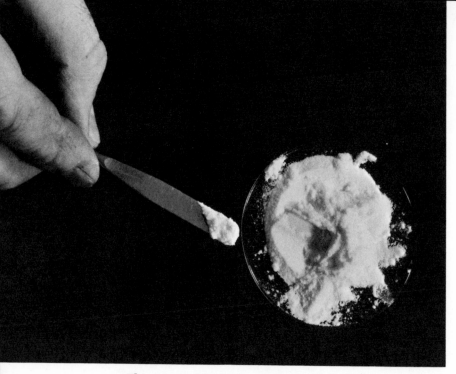

This insect virus is in experimental use in the control of corn ear worms, cotton boll worms, and tobacco bud worms. It occurs naturally and is biodegradable (breaks down naturally into harmless substances).

new biochemical approach called *juvenile hormone.* This is a natural biological substance that mixes up the growth and development cycles of specific insects, leaving the others untouched.

What else can be done to save our environment? We must begin to question whether growth is always good. There is a large indicator in the lobby of a government building in Washington, D.C. It shows an up-to-date figure for the rate at which our economy is "running." This is the Gross National Product, the total of all goods and services produced in the country. Recently this figure topped one trillion dollars for the first time in our history. There was something of a celebration.

180

Yet, also for the first time in our history, there is a nagging feeling in the hearts of some of us that unbridled growth is perhaps not all it is cracked up to be.

Not only must we begin to consider the possibilities of keeping down the rate of population growth but we must also begin to wonder whether more television sets, more air conditioners, and more cars for each of us are really necessary, or even desirable. For it takes much energy to produce these items and to keep them running. Similarly, although fewer farmers are producing far more than in years past, they are in a sense making up for it by using far more energy in the form of fuel than they did years ago.

There is already talk of serious fuel shortages in the northeast in the near future. And, of course, greater energy production means more air, and perhaps water, pollution. It has already been found that even low-level air pollution can hurt crops. The Ehrlichs report that "if current trends continue, California will not be able to feed herself much longer, let alone export food."

And Lester R. Brown maintains that "the average North American currently makes about four times as great a demand on the earth's agricultural ecosystem as someone living in one of the poor countries" (e.g., in the indirect and inefficient consumption of grains by livestock). As the LDCs become more developed, their inhabitants are certain to want to live as we do, and of course they have every right to. But the United States, with about only one-twentieth of the world's population, uses something like half of the world's resources. Clearly, if everyone in the world wanted, and could afford, to live this way, serious shortages of natural resources would develop very quickly. Already there are impending shortages of some metals. We must be careful, therefore, of the dangers of "exporting" our way of doing things. Or, we must change our own ways, which makes more sense.

FEEDING
THE WORLD OF THE FUTURE

Feeding the world of the future presents similar problems. World population is expected to double in the next few decades. But we can now foresee a requirement for a tripling of grain production and a quadrupling of meat production. This is because as the LDCs improve their conditions, the people therein will want to eat better as well as more. Some of these additional requirements may of course be met by one or more of the developments we have discussed.

Recycling

A very important contribution to maintaining the environment will be the increased recycling of wastes and other by-products. This is certainly not a new idea. For a long time garbage was fed to pigs and other livestock, for example. There are dangers with this, however, such as the possibility of disease in the livestock from tainted foods. But it may be possible to sterilize the garbage, perhaps with atomic radiation. Or perhaps we can feed the garbage to algae or bacteria, and the resultant SCP to the animals.

We consume millions of tons of wood a year in the manufacture of paper. Although reforestation methods are being practiced we are still losing forests all over the country. Yet a considerable part of these needs could be supplied from agricultural waste products. Corn stalks, oat hulls, sugar cane, and wheat waste all contain the same kind of cellulose that is contained in wood and is basic to the production of paper. Although the yield might not be as great, it might pay in the long run. Certainly, it would be better from an ecological point of view. The land saved could go into food production if necessary.

An important question is, who is going to do this? If the paper companies can make more money by using wood,

182

why should they get involved with the expense and complication of using agricultural (or other) waste? After all, they are in the business to make money; their stockholders might not like the idea of lowered profits, even for a good cause. The best approach would be to develop methods which would make the use of waste products practical and economical. Should that not be possible, incentives (or perhaps penalties) should be instituted by the government to insure that these processes are used anyway.

It would be ecologically useful to arrange things so that producing in a wasteful way becomes more, not less, costly. Perhaps the cost of raw materials will have to include a provision for disposal.

Here are a few other examples of how agricultural wastes can be, or have been, used:

Vegetable and fruit processing plants in Pennsylvania produce about a quarter of a million tons of waste a year. M. L. Borger of Pennsylvania State University estimates that this tonnage could support 25,000 head of cattle for a full year.

LSU engineers break open bales of sugar cane pulp called baghasse at the university's pilot plant where it will be converted into protein by microbial action.

Chicken litter contains up to 30 per cent protein and can be used as part of the feed requirements for cattle.

Researchers at Ohio State are feeding treated and pelletized garbage to cattle and sheep. Thus far results are encouraging.

In what is perhaps the most advanced concept, a farm has been proposed for the heart of Alaska, where the temperature sometimes drops to 70° below zero. The basic idea is to recycle hog wastes—to treat and supplement these wastes and then feed them to the pigs. These wastes would go back as about 10 per cent of the hogs' feed, with the balance being supplied by barley grown elsewhere on the farm. Here too the wastes would be used, in this case as fertilizer. And certainly other uses could be found for the wastes as well. State Senator Ed Merdes suggests that if a true waste-free hog raising facility can be developed it may be possible to put multi-story "farms" near cities, thus solving distribution and transportation problems.

It may also be feasible to utilize city and industrial wastes in positive ways. For instance waste paper in the United States alone runs to some 35 million tons a year. Some of this is recycled into new paper. But a great deal is not. The telephone company is having trouble getting buyers for its old directories. The result is that in New York City, for example, the telephone company no longer retrieves the old directories when it delivers the new ones. The old books were once used to make new paper; now they make up a 22,000-ton-per-year burden on an already overloaded solid-waste disposal system.

On an even larger scale, solid wastes from all cities and towns in the United States add up to more than three billion tons a year, of which at least half is cellulose-containing material such as paper, rags, leaves, boxes, wood, etc. The cellulose is the chief constituent of plant cell walls.

184

Cellulose can be converted to protein if it is first broken down into glucose, a sugar, and then fermented. But because the cellulose does not break down easily, paper, rags, and wood can, under some circumstances, last for hundreds and even thousands of years. Among the methods being tested to aid in this breakdown are chemicals, nuclear radiation, lasers, and microorganisms.

Termites, for example, have a microorganism in their bodies which enables them to digest wood. Perhaps we could feed cows some *Trichonympha* or otherwise get it into their digestive systems, and then somehow get them to eat sawdust or even wood chips.

We have already seen that cattle can be fed with a mixture containing a substantial amount of waste paper—as much as

Dairy cow tastes novel, nutritious feed made of ground-up newspapers and molasses.

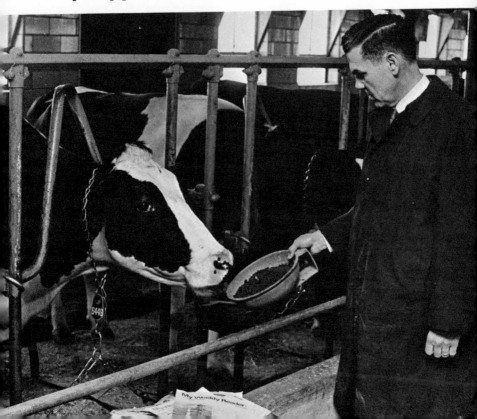

31.6 per cent, in one experiment. The rest of the mixture consisted of 48.3 per cent molasses and 20.1 per cent soybean meal. A control group was fed a standard mixture of 75 per cent ground shelled corn, 22 per cent soybean meal, and 2 per cent minerals. Although the test animals did not gain as much weight as the control group (about 1.7 pounds a day vs. about 2.5), there are no health problems and they were quite fit otherwise. Perhaps, in the future, if it becomes accepted that waste paper can be used to feed cattle, then livestock farmers will have to be charged for not using waste paper in their feed. In this way the cost of society's having to dispose of the waste paper in other ways will be included in the raising of grain-fed cattle. This may sound unfair, even ridiculous to the farmers. Obviously, the rate of production of waste paper should also be curtailed. My only objective is to indicate that we shall have to search out all kinds of new solutions.

Ultimately, it is conceivable that no food will have to be (or will be allowed to be) raised especially for animal feed. By the use of various processing techniques we might be able to feed them almost entirely on waste material, thus freeing a great deal of prime land for human food, housing, recreation, or whatever.

This is a pure strain of thermophilic bacteria (tiny rod-shaped objects) digesting waste cellulose and converting it into microbial protein.

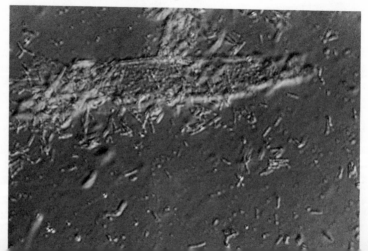

We have already seen that microorganisms can exist on petroleum products. Perhaps, when SCP becomes an important part of our diets, we can also feed the microorganisms on such delicacies as the acid-liquid residues of paper processing, fish wastes, old railroad ties, and discarded rubber tires; all of these have already been shown, at least experimentally, to be edible by these organisms. And, finally, in the manner reminiscent of the Indian's use of dung for cooking fuel, a Maxwell House Coffee plant is using spent coffee grounds from making instant coffee as a fuel for making more instant coffee.

Sewage

Another major factor in our environmental system is water; while our concern in this book is mainly with water as an aid in growing crops and as a medium for growing seafood, it is also of course essential to other aspects of our daily lives as well. A clean, pollution-free water supply is obviously necessary for our continued existence.

Yet Lyndon Johnson said back in the 1960's that every major river system in the United States was already polluted. Fertilizer, top soil, and pesticide run-off from farms, chemicals from industry, and sewage from cities and towns have all combined to do this to what not too long ago was a system of crystal-clear water.

More careful management of farms can prevent much of the offending run-off. And strict laws and taxes can prevent much of the chemical pollution though probably not all of it. The sewage problem is an especially difficult one, for we ourselves produce the sewage that is often pumped directly into our rivers, lakes, and seas. If this is allowed to go on, we may very well make all of them unlivable, in which case

187

we can forget about getting food from the sea; and if we make the water undrinkable as well, we can forget about everything.

R. Buckminster Fuller, inventor/architect/thinker, has a way of putting things very clearly and succinctly. He writes:

> If you are in a shipwreck and all of the boats are gone, and a piano top comes along that is buoyant enough to keep you afloat, it makes a fortuitous life preserver. But this is not to say that the best way to design a life preserver is in the form of a piano top. I think that we—as society—are clinging to a great many piano tops . . .*

In other words, we need to investigate entirely new ways of doing things. We must, for one thing, change from a cowboy to a spaceman economy. Let me explain. We have mentioned two problems, for instance; an overly heavy input of chemicals into our land and a contamination of our water supplies with substances that contain a high proportion of what could be useful materials, if put to proper use. Isn't it possible to combine these two problems so that they take care of each other? That is, can't we reuse some or all of the materials on the land that we are now throwing into the water?

This is the basic meaning of a spaceman economy. The spaceman *must* conserve his resources; he cannot afford to throw anything out. So he must reuse everything he possibly can. One suggestion has been that on long trips he carry along a culture of algae. The idea is that he can use his own wastes as food for the algae, which he can then eat.

Sounds terrible, doesn't it? But it must be remembered that human and other wastes consist of basic elements. When

* "An Operating Manual for Spaceship Earth," in *Environment and Change, the Next Fifty Years,* W. R. Ewald, Jr., ed., Indiana University Press, 1968, p. 342.

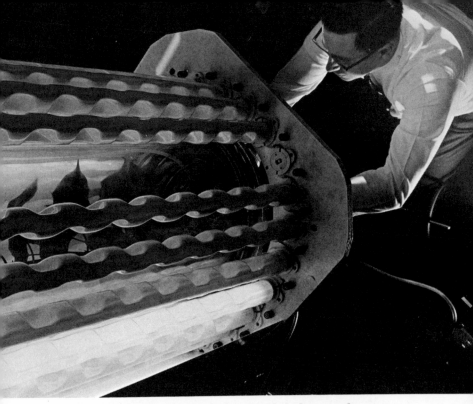

At Battelle Memorial Institute broad-leafed plants, such
as the sweet potato shown here, are being evaluated as
a source of oxygen and food for astronauts in the
closed environment of a space station.

these are broken down and made into a different material,
they are just that, a different material. Further, the description given above is highly simplified. It may be necessary,
for example (if only for psychological reasons), to use two
stages of algae, the second fed with something other than
human waste. Something similar is sometimes done on feed
lots: the garbage fed to pigs, or certain kinds of fish meal
fed to cattle may cause an unpleasant odor in the meat. So
the fattening-up process is finished off with a higher grade
of less objectionable food, and the final product, the meat,
is perfectly acceptable in spite of the fact that the majority

189

of the weight gain came from garbage or other unpleasant substances.

In a cowboy economy, on the other hand, all wastes are simply thrown away, which is pretty much what we do today. In the conversion from a cowboy to a spaceman economy, one of the most important steps would be to somehow use the sewage we now pump into our water systems. Various experiments are being carried on in various parts of the world in attempts to do just this. In one of the more advanced, Penn State has actually been spraying treated sewage water over crop and forest land for several years. To date, some 500,000 gallons of waste water have been used daily; this represents about 16 per cent of the waste water from the university sewage plant. The water is also used to irrigate athletic fields and other open spaces.

Dr. Louis T. Kardos, professor of soil technology at the university, says that relatively small amounts of land are required. Thus only about 1,300 acres would be enough to dispose of the water from a city of 100,000. Further, the

Eight years of spray irrigation using waste water at The Pennsylvania State University has shown significant increases in crop production and tree and forest growth with no harmful effects.

growth of the plants and trees was quite satisfactory. Plans are to increase the size of the system so that it can handle the entire output of the university and the nearby town of State College.

In other experiments, it has been found that

a) the sewage from a community of 10,000, used over a 130 acre test area, doubled the yield of corn and tripled the yield of hay

b) sewage sludge, the solids remaining after the water is treated, is rich in nutrients and can be converted to a syrup-like molasses for use as an animal feed (Foster D. Snell, Inc.)

c) edible algae can be produced as a bonus in a waste-water treatment plant (Rutgers University)

d) the sludge can also be used directly as fertilizer and/or livestock feed (with processing)

e) sewage sludge can be mixed with sand and soil and used to fill in bays and lagoons, creating new areas containing rich soil

f) sludge gas, created in the processing, can be burned to supply heat and power

The list of possibilities is endless.

The next step is to change things that *can* be done to things that *are* done. And this, in a sense, is even harder to accomplish. There is the established way of doing things—the cowboy approach. We have all been brought up that way, and it is not easy to change long-standing habits.

In my town, Leonia, New Jersey, we recycle waste paper, glass and aluminum cans. It is a bit more trouble for the householder to separate these items and to bring the glass and aluminum to a central collection point once a month or to set out the papers for collection. But those of us who do it feel we are making a contribution to keeping the refuse problem from getting entirely out of hand. It must be mentioned, however, that so far the labor of collection has been done on a volunteer basis. The profits from selling the waste materials go to local organizations.

Perhaps the next step will be separation of food wastes, which will be processed and fed to livestock kept in nearby "bacon bins."

Or, if these are put into "compost piles" and mixed with good soil they are decomposed by soil organisms and eventually make a fine organic fertilizer and soil conditioner. Each town or district may eventually have to have one; or each homeowner may be required to have his own.

A distinct possibility is that if we are not careful enough now, we may do so much damage to the environment that we will cause an eventual *decrease* in our food production capability.

Agricultural and food industry executives point proudly to the enormous variety of our foods and to the fact that we spend less for our food than any other country on earth. But do we really? How much are we also spending—and how much will we have to spend in the future—on cleaning up the mess that is being made in the growing and processing of that food? A realistic approach now will save much trouble later.

This is an important point and bears restating. There is little question that the world can produce food for two, five, or even ten times the present population.

But, as Lester Brown points out in an article in *Scientific American*, "The central question is no longer 'Can we produce enough food?' but 'What are the environmental consequences of attempting to do so?'"

192

Epilogue

THERE IS AN OLD CHINESE PROVERB: if you give a man a fish, you feed him for a day; if you teach him how to fish, you feed him for a lifetime.

The United States and other DCs have given out many "fish" over the last few decades. The question now is, what are they doing about helping the LDCs to fish for themselves —and why should they bother?

Consider this situation. Grain production is going up in the LDCs. This is fine for the LDCs; but it also means that the DCs are beginning to lose their own grain markets. This is not making our farmers happy. And when the farmers are not happy, their congressmen are not happy.

If the poor countries can begin to produce grain at a lower price than we can, for instance, then grain dealers will naturally tend to import this new grain from LDCs rather than buy it locally. The usual way of trying to prevent this is called protectionism. Our government (or that of any DC) institutes import quotas (limitations) and taxes which make the imported grain more expensive than our own. This is what we mean by protectionism; our government is "protecting" the grain farmer.

193

But this is short-sighted thinking; and it can stop the Green Revolution in its tracks. Professor D. G. Johnson of the University of Chicago estimates that merely "changing the trade and agricultural policies of the developed nations could easily result in an annual $1-billion increase in the foreign exchange earnings of the developing nations." By foreign exchange earnings we mean the money and credit earned by the commodities they sell on the world market. They desperately need these earnings to help them buy seed, fertilizer, tools, machinery, and so on.

The unfortunate truth of the matter is that we in the DCs are apparently not eager to accept the LDCs as competitors on the world grain market. The 1960's, believe it or not, constituted a decade of *increasing* protectionism, in grains and other products as well. Among other crops that are protected are rice, peanuts, and certain fruits and vegetables that are better and more easily grown in LDCs. We did not loosen up and help the LDCs along these lines; rather we made things more difficult for them on the free market.

We must not use our greater economic strength to beat them in the economic battlefield. We must be willing to pitch in with more than token contributions of surplus food, seed and fertilizer. It may mean that we as a country will have to tighten our belts a bit. This is something that must be realized, and faced realistically. (In a step in the right direction, the European Common Market countries have agreed to remove import duties from manufactured and semi-manufactured goods produced in LDCs.)

Why?

For some, the question will immediately arise—why? Why should we have to tighten our belts? Why should we voluntarily give up a hard-earned competitive advantage?

194

The simple answer is that if we don't, and if we make it difficult or impossible for the LDCs to earn the foreign exchange they so desperately need, the end result will be that they will never complete the changeover from LDC to DC. And that would be a catastrophe, for a number of reasons.

First of course is the humanitarian one. Some people may sit by and do nothing out of greed. If the rich nations continue to get richer and the poor ones poorer, then a feeling begins to grow that because the people in the LDCs are so "different" (uneducated, rural, etc.), they are somehow less human than we are. This can lead to only half-hearted efforts to help. All of us, however, become brutalized if we sit by and allow people to succumb to disease and starvation.

Helping the LDCs to increase output per unit of land will help feed hungry people; but it will still leave the workers poor. Somehow the output per worker must increase. This can only be done through investment in better seeds, livestock, fertilizer, machinery, energy sources, etc. And the LDCs need foreign exchange for that.

But there are positive reasons why we should help as well. One is that when and if the LDCs become DCs, then new customers will be created for our more expensive products, just as we are a good market for expensive cars, watches, and so forth from other countries.

Another reason is that political instability is lessened.

A third is that almost anything we do to prevent malnutrition elsewhere, particularly in terms of research, will help us accomplish the same here.

And, finally, this is a great challenge. We have risen to great challenges before—in two nearly catastrophic world wars, for example. Perhaps we can do the same in a more constructive vein.

What can the average person do? He can encourage his congressman to be open-minded about world cooperation, even if it means a bit of belt-tightening at home.

Young people particularly can help by becoming interested in the problem and perhaps looking into the possibilities of specializing in some field or aspect of agricultural science. Not every agricultural expert can win a Nobel Prize, as Dr. Borlaug did, but there is much that can be, and still needs to be, done. One of the problems with the Peace Corps is that we have had too few such experts to send overseas. The best-willed liberal arts major is of little help when faced with an unyielding soil. As a laborer, he is certainly no great addition to a local economy; the LDCs have all the labor they need.

No, what they need are technical experts, first to help them directly, and second to teach them how to do these things for themselves. Someone must be able to determine the feasibility, cost, and design of irrigation systems; evaluate the potential fertility of a soil and what is needed in the way of fertilizer and soil conditioners to bring it up to maximum productive efficiency; supervise construction of roads; purchase *useful* farm machinery and set up maintenance and repair procedures; handle credit arrangements for importing or producing hardware, fertilizer, or other farm aids; and so on. A nutrition-improvement program may require the services of irrigation, road and agricultural specialists, veterinarians, nutritionists, plant and animal disease specialists, chemical engineers, along with economists, market experts, and even food processing and transportation experts.

Strangely enough, we are short of agricultural experts even here in our own country. Agricultural science has to a large extent given way to the more "glamorous" fields—chemistry, biology, physics, electronics.

In the LDCs, however, the shortage is calamitous. Professor James Bonner of the California Institute of Technology says

196

that in 1957 only 10 trained agriculturalists were produced in all of Africa. All of Latin America produced only 750; that figure had risen to only 1,100 ten years later. Tiny Japan, in contrast, produces more than 7,000 graduate agriculturalists per year.

In some of the countries the problem is illiteracy. Only a few per cent of the children in Ethiopia and Malawi of high school age are in school.

But even in those countries with a higher literacy rate, there is another, perhaps even more difficult, problem to lick. While there may be an established school system, the emphasis is often wrong. In any LDC the greatest need is for technical-level people, such as agriculturalists, but few of these are produced. Yet in India, for example, there are plenty of university graduates. The same is true of such places as Egypt, Latin America and, to a lesser extent, Africa. Unfortunately, few of these graduates have taken practical courses of study. They have for the most part majored in liberal arts or in the more glamorous areas of science and technology—for which there is as yet little need in the LDCs. So, many of them emigrate to the DCs, where their talents can be used.

The problem, of course, is two-fold. First, world-wide communications have convinced many of those who can go to college that they are living in a modern world, so of course they want to study the more advanced, more glamorous fields, just as our own students want to. The difference is that we can afford this, while they can't.

The second aspect has to do with the fact that many of the LDCs were for many years colonies of the Western countries, and their educational systems were designed after those of the West, even though the needs were altogether different.

197

We still have a problem understanding that the economics and needs of LDCs are different from DCs and will therefore require quite different solutions. Here we think in terms of labor-saving devices. In the LDCs, we must think of labor-*creating* methods and devices.

Can it Be Done?

The final question: Can it be done? Can the LDCs be brought up to the point of higher development? To the point where they can not only feed themselves but enter into the mainstream of modern life?

Perhaps we should recall that both Australia and the United States, both of which now produce food in great abundance, were, not very long ago, LDCs themselves. Many early settlements had to be abandoned because of lack of food. Today, many farmers in the United States and elsewhere are paid *not* to produce food.

The big difference, of course, is vastly larger populations. Dr. Borlaug, whom we mentioned earlier, should know something about the situation; he is seriously concerned, and constantly points out, that whatever has been accomplished in the Green Revolution is threatened and even negated by more hungry children. "All we've really done," he says, "is buy time, maybe 20 or 30 years. We have instilled hope where there was complete despair. But every time the clock ticks there are 2.2 more mouths to feed. The ticking keeps eroding away what progress we've been able to make."

Among the problems that must be overcome is the large families that result from farmers feeling that they need a few sons to help out. As we noted earlier, because of the fear of starvation and disease they have larger families than they actually need, as a sort of "cushion."

198

One reason for this is that the farmers haven't gotten used to the fact that they are less likely to lose children through disease than they used to, because of better medical care, drugs, and sanitation. The final result is even larger families than there used to be.

Thus, strange though it may seem, it is very likely that more food and a better standard of living could eventually mean fewer people later on. For once the farmer begins to believe that he can feed himself and even earn some extra cash with only his own labor, then and only then will the size of the large families now being raised be reduced.

As is to be expected, there are some who question this idea, namely that better nutrition will help lower the birth rate. Certainly, however, the present situation of hunger and malnutrition is *not* lowering it.

Professor Thayer Scudder, of the California Institute of Technology, feels that "you have to produce an education explosion—for both population control and agricultural development—that goes faster than the population explosion, before you can put the brakes on."

If so, we had better begin doing more than we have been doing, and soon. The regional international research institutes are a good start, but no more than that. One estimate is that we need fifty such institutes spaced around the world. The total cost of building and staffing them, assuming we find the people, would be surprisingly small—at least when compared to food aid and various other forms of direct assistance. The total cost might run to perhaps $3 billion. That is a lot of money. But consider the alternative.

The governments of the LDCs will have to make some changes too. In some of the countries, as in South America, for instance, vast estates are handed down from generation to generation, making for a few rich and many poor who have little hope for the future. Too many of these poor farmers are not sharing in the Green Revolution. Something will have to be done for them, but their own governments will have to do this.

Some would urge a simpler attack. Why not, they say, just produce all we can and then give away the surplus. The answer is that if we do, we are just giving the LDCs a "fish." Their peoples will forever remain dependent, angry, ashamed. Another unpleasant result of this disposing of surplus foods is that production of food in the LDCs is thereby discouraged rather than encouraged; prices are depressed as well. Giving a country food (except in terms of emergency aid) does it no good whatever.

No, there seems no way around it. The LDCs will have to do the job themselves, though with our help.

Workers in West Bengal, India, on a flood control and irrigation project, receive CARE food as wages.

Epilogue

The contributions of the DCs will be:

Continue to provide emergency food aid

Provide research institutions, training aids, experienced personnel, and funds

Maintain more equitable (helpful) trade policies

The jobs of the LDCs:

Slow the rate of population increase

Produce an increasing quantity and quality of food

Find a way of distributing land and food more equitably

Somehow, somewhere the way to accomplish all of this must be figured out. Hopefully, if we can pull some of the LDCs up onto their feet, they can find the answers for the others. In the meantime we must do everything we can to help.

Appendix A

Selected Careers in Agriculture and Related Fields

Agricultural Consultant
Agricultural Broker
Agricultural Economist
Agricultural Engineer
Agricultural Instructor
Agricultural Missionary
Agricultural Editor
Agricultural Salesman
Aerial Applicator
Agronomist
Animal Specialist
Bacteriologist
Banking Official
Beekeeper
Biochemist
Biologist

Biophysicist
Botanist
Breeding Technician
College Faculty Member
Commodity Grader
Conservationist
County Extension Agent
Dairyman
Dairy Plant Manager
Dairy Technologist
Director of Research
Electric Farm Advisor
Electric Plant Manager
Elevator Manager
Farm Appraiser
Farm Equipment Specialist

Selected Careers in Agriculture
and Related Fields

Farm Machinery Dealer
Farm Manager
Farm Planner
Feed Dealer
Feed Technologist
Field Representative
Food Processor
Food Technologist
Forester
Fruit Grower
Geneticist—Plant or Animal
Grain Buyer
Horticulturist
Inspector—Food or Feed
Insurance Broker
Livestock Breeder
Livestock Feeder

Nurseryman
Nutritionist—Plant—Animal
Organizational Fieldman
Pathologist—Plant—Animal
Physiologist
Poultryman
Quality Control Specialist
Rancher
Rural Sociologist
Seed Grower
Seed Broker
Soil Scientist
Vegetable Grower
Veterinarian
Wildlife Specialist
Zoologist

Source: Agricultural Marketing Group, Edison Electric Institute, 750 Third Avenue, New York, N.Y. 10017.

Appendix B

The Top Ten Colleges and Universities in Agricultural Enrollment in the United States

Iowa State U.	U. of California
Ohio State U.	U. of Minnesota
Purdue U.	U. of Missouri
Cornell U.	Oklahoma State U.
Texas A & M	Michigan State U.

Source: *Pathways of Knowledge 1968*, University of Missouri, 1969.

For a more complete list of colleges and universities giving degrees in agriculture and related fields, see the section called "Professional and Special Programs—Where to Find Them," in *Lovejoy's College Guide*, published by Simon & Schuster and available in most libraries. Note particularly the listings under the following fields:

Agriculture

Agronomy, Field Crops

Animal Science

Bacteriology, Virology and
   Mycology

Beef Cattle Raising

Citrus Fruit Farming and
   Processing

Dairy Science

Engineering, Agricultural

Food Processing Technology

Food Technology

*Home Economics, Foods and
   Nutrition

Marine Biology and Fisheries

Poultry Husbandry

Soil Science

Bibliography

BOOKS

Aldrich, D. G., Jr., ed. *Research for the World Food Crisis.* American Association for the Advancement of Science, 1970.

Asimov, Isaac. *Life and Energy.* Doubleday, 1962.

Bardach, J. E. *Harvest of the Sea.* Harper & Row, 1968.

Bardach, J. E., and Ryther, J. H. *The Status and Potential of Aquaculture.* Springfield, Va., Clearinghouse for Federal Scientific and Technical Information, 1968.

Beckwith, B. P. *The Next 500 Years.* Exposition Press, Inc., 1967.

Bellerby, J. R., ed. *Factory Farming.* London, Education Services, 1970.

Bicknell, F. *Chemicals in Your Food.* Emerson Books, 1961.

Bieber, Herman, ed. *Engineering of Unconventional Protein Production.* American Institute of Chemical Engineers, 1969.

Brown, L. R. *Seeds of Change, The Green Revolution and Development in the 1970's.* Praeger, 1970.

Calder, Nigel, ed. *The World in 1984.* Vols. 1 and 2. Pelican, 1965.

Charley, Helen. *Food Science.* Ronald Press, 1971.

Cockrane, W. W. *The World Food Problem—a Guardedly Optimistic View.* Crowell, 1969.

Dumont, R., and Rosier, B. *The Hungry Future.* Praeger, 1969.

Edlin, H. L. *Plants and Man; The Story of Our Basic Food.* Natural History Press, 1969.

Ehrlich, P. R. *The Population Bomb.* Ballantine, 1968.

Ehrlich, P. R., and A. H. *Population, Resources, Environment, Issues in Human Ecology.* Freeman, 1970.

Elting, M., and Folsom, M. *The Mysterious Grain, Science in Search of the Origin of Corn.* M. Evans, 1967.

Esterer, A. H. *Food, Riches of the Earth,* Messner, 1969.

Falk, Irving A., ed. *Prophecy for the Year 2000.* Messner, 1970.

Food and Agriculture Organization of the United Nations. *Indicative World Plan for Agricultural Development.* Vols. I, II, and III. August 1969.

Bibliography

——. *The State of World Fisheries: World Food Problems,* #7. 1968.

Food and Agriculture Organization/International Atomic Energy Agency. *Elimination of Harmful Organisms From Food and Feed by Irradiation.* Proceedings of a panel, distributed by National Agency for International Publications, Inc., 1967.

——. *Induced Mutations in Plants.* Proceedings of a symposium, distributed by National Agency for International Publications, Inc., 1969.

——. *New Approaches to Breeding for Improved Plant Protein.* Proceedings of a panel, distributed by National Agency for International Publications, Inc., 1969.

——. *Rice Breeding with Induced Mutations.* Technical Reports Series No. 102, distributed by National Agency for International Publications, Inc., 1970.

Foreign Policy Association. *Toward the Year 2018.* Cowles Education Corp., 1968.

Freeman, O. L. *World Without Hunger.* Praeger, 1968.

Furnas, C. C. *The Next Hundred Years.* Regnal & Hitchcock, 1936.

Galston, A. W. *The Life of the Green Plant.* Prentice-Hall, 1961.

Ganschow, Cliff, ed. *1971 Ford Almanac, Farm and Home Edition.* Golden Press, 1971

Good, I. J., ed. *The Scientist Speculates: An Anthology of Partly-Baked Ideas.* Basic. 1962.

Halacy, D. S., Jr. *Century 21: Your Life in the Year 2001 and Beyond.* Macrae Smith, 1968.

Hardin, C., ed. *Overcoming World Hunger.* Prentice-Hall, 1969.

Hayes, Jack, ed. *Contours of Change. 1970 Yearbook of Agriculture.* U.S. Department of Agriculture, available through U.S. Government Printing Office.

——. *Protecting Our Food. 1966 Yearbook of Agriculture.* U.S. Department of Agriculture, available through U.S. Government Printing Office.

——. *Science for Better Living. 1968 Yearbook of Agriculture.* U.S. Department of Agriculture, available through U.S. Government Printing Office.

Hollings, E. F. *The Case Against Hunger: A Demand for a National Policy.* Cowles, 1970.

Idyll, C. P. *The Sea Against Hunger.* Crowell, 1970.

Johnson, L. S. *What We Eat; The Origins and Travels of Foods Around the World.* Rand McNally, 1969.

Katz, N. *Let Them Eat Promises: The Politics of Hunger in America.* Prentice-Hall, 1970.

Little, E. C. S. *Handbook of Utilization of Aquatic Plants.* Food and Agriculture Organization of the United Nations, 1968.

Lowenberg, M. E., et al. *Food and Man.* Wiley, 1968.

McCormack, Arthur. *The Population Problem.* Crowell, 1970.

Marx, W. *The Frail Ocean,* Coward-McCann, 1967.

Mateles, R. I., and Tannenbaum, S. R., eds. *Single Cell Protein.* M.I.T., 1968.

Office for Industrial Associates. *The Next Ninety Years.* Proceedings of a conference, California Institute of Technology, 1967.

Olson, T. A., and Burgess, F. J., eds. *Pollution and Marine Ecology.* Interscience, 1967.

Pirie, N. W. *Food Resources, Conventional and Unconventional.* Pelican, 1969.

Scott, John. *Hunger: A Background on Man's Struggle to Feed Himself.* Parents Magazine Press, 1969.

Smith, Anthony. *The Body.* Walker, 1968.

Stakman, E. C., et al. *Campaigns Against Hunger.* Harvard University Press, 1967.

Stefferud, A. *Farmer's World, 1964 Yearbook of Agriculture.* U.S. Department of Agriculture, available through U.S. Government Printing Office.

Still, Henry. *Man: The Next 30 Years.* Hawthorne, 1968.

Tannenbaum, B., and Stillman, M. *Understanding Food: The Chemistry of Nutrition.* McGraw-Hill, 1962.

Thomson, George. *The Foreseeable Future.* Cambridge University Press, 1955.

Turner, J. S. *The Chemical Feast.* Grossman, 1970. (The Ralph Nader Study Group Report on Food Protection and the Food and Drug Administration.)

Staff. *Here Comes Tomorrow.* Dow Jones Books, 1966, 1967.

Wells, G. S. *Garden in the West: A Dramatic Account of Science in Agriculture.* Dodd, Mead, 1969.

PAMPHLETS, BOOKLETS, REPORTS

Agricultural Experiment Station. *Odyssey into the Eighties.* University of Minnesota, n.d.

–––. " 'Tailor-Made' Vegetables." Special edition of *Michigan Science in Action,* Michigan State University, June 1970.

Albrecht, H. R. *Problems of Tropical Agriculture.* A Ford Foundation Reprint from *Standard Bank Review,* May 1970.

Beaumariage, D. S. *Manufacture of Fish Meal From Florida's Fishery Waste and Underexploited Fishes.* Technical Series No. 54, Florida Board of Conservation Marine Laboratory (St. Petersburg, Florida), April 1968.

Bird, Kermit. "The Food Processing Front of the Seventies." Paper presented to the American Dietetic Association, U.S. Department of Agriculture, October 8, 1970.

Caster, W. O., ed. *Hunger and Malnutrition in Georgia, 1969.* Report #1 of the Inter-Institutional Committee on Nutrition, University of Georgia.

Department of Nutrition and Food Science. *List of Publications.* Two volumes: May 1, 1968–March 31, 1970; March 30, 1970–April 8, 1971. Massachusetts Institute of Technology.

Bibliography

Dull, G. G., ed. *The Food Problem in Georgia.* Report #2 of the Inter-Institutional Committee on Nutrition, University of Georgia, 1970.

Environmental Research Laboratory. *Progress Report on the Development of a System for the Production of Power, Water and Food in Coastal Desert Areas, and the Development of a Large Scale Controlled Environment Research Facility for Agricultural Production.* University of Arizona, May 1970.

Food and Agriculture Organization of the United Nations. *Five Keys To Development.* 1970.

———. *Food Losses: The Tragedy . . . and Some Solutions,* n.d.

———. *A Strategy for Plenty, the Indicative World Plan for Agricultural Development.* 1970.

———. *World Food Program,* n.d.

Ford Foundation. *A Richer Harvest, A Report on Ford Foundation Grants in Overseas Agriculture.* October 1967.

———. *Sowing the Green Revolution, International Institute of Tropical Agriculture.* April 1970.

Grosser, M. "The Control of Insects." *Zoecon Corporation 1970 Annual Report* (Palo Alto, California), 1970.

International Minerals and Chemicals. *Growth Sciences, The Immediate Beyond.* 1965.

———. *The Quiet Revolution, A Call for Action in World Agriculture.* n.d.

Laine, B., and Shacklady, C. A. *Production and Utilization of BP Protein Concentrate.* British

Petroleum Company, Ltd., 1967.

Litchfield, J. H. "Nutrition in Life Support Systems for Space Exploration." Reprint from *Proceedings of the Seventh International Congress of Nutrition,* available from Battelle Memorial Institute, Columbus, Ohio, 1966.

Mead, Margaret, ed. *Hunger.* Scientists' Institute for Public Information, 1970.

Murphy, W. B. *A Practical View of Future Food Problems.* Campbell Soup Company (Camden, New Jersey), 1965.

National Center for Health Statistics. *Height and Weight of Children in the United States, India, and the United Arab Republic.* U.S. Department of Health, Education and Welfare, available through U.S. Government Printing Office, 1970.

Oak Ridge National Laboratory. *Nuclear Energy Centers, Industrial and Agro-Industrial Complexes Summary Report,* March 1969.

Snyder, D. G. *Fish Protein Concentrate: A History of Its Commercial Development (Summary).* Bureau of Commercial Fisheries, U.S. Department of the Interior (College Park, Maryland), n.d.

Union Carbide. *For a World of Plenty: The Role of Pest Control in Our High Standard of Living.* 1963.

United States Congress. *Food for Peace.* 1969 Annual Report in Public Law 480, June 1970. Available through U.S. Government Printing Office.

Universidad de Sonora/University of Arizona. *Power/Water/Food Experiments at Puerto Peñasco* (in Spanish and English). n.d.

University of Miami Sea Grant Institution Program. *Aquaculture: The New Shrimp Crop.* Sea Grant Information Leaflet, February 1970.

Vision-17, Inc. *Century 21: A Symposium on the Future of the Small Community.* Doane College, n.d.

ARTICLES

Agrawal, Harish. "Revolution in The Fields." *New Scientist,* August 29, 1968.

Altschul, A. M. "Food Proteins: New Sources From Seeds." *Science,* October 13, 1967.

Auerbach, C. "The Chemical Production of Mutations." *Science,* December 1967.

Bachman, W. A. "Protein from Oil Starts its Move Out of Research Lab." *The Oil and Gas Journal,* February 26, 1968.

Bardach, J. E. "Agriculture." *Science,* September 13, 1968.

Baron, S. "Cheaper Than the Tractor." *Ceres, the FAO Review,* March–April 1968.

Billard, J. B. "The Revolution in American Agriculture." *National Geographic,* February 1970.

Block, V. "Tomorrow's New Foods." *Science Digest,* January 1967.

Boerma, A. H. "A World Agricultural Plan." *Scientific American,* August 1970.

Borlaug, Norman. "The Green Revolution." *Bulletin of the Atomic Scientists,* June 1971.

Bramao, D. L. "Making Better Use of the World's Soils." *Ceres, the FAO Review,* March–April 1968.

"Breeding Carp with Fewer Bones." *Science Digest,* February 1971.

Brown, K. V. "Whale Farming in a Coral Corral." *Science Digest,* December 1968.

Brown, L. R. "Human Food Production as a Process in the Biosphere." *Scientific American,* September 1970.

———. "Nobel Peace Prize: Developer of High-Yield Wheat Receives Award." *Science,* October 30, 1970.

———. "The World Outlook for Conventional Agriculture." *Science,* November 3, 1967.

Byerly, T. C. "Efficiency of Feed Conversion." *Science,* August 25, 1967.

Byrnes, F. C. "A Matter of Life and Death." *Rockefeller Foundation Quarterly,* January 1969.

Call, D. L. "The Impact of Meat Analogs." *Meat,* January 1968.

Cancino, R., and Lawhon, J. T. "A Look at Unconventional Sources of Protein." *The Cotton Gin and Oil Mill Press,* May 30, 1970.

Cathey, H. M., et al. "Chemical Pruning of Plants." *Science,* September 16, 1966.

Chase, S. S. "Anti-Famine Strategy: Genetic Engineering for Food." *Bulletin of the Atomic Scientists,* October 1969.

Clawson, et al. "Desalted Water for Agriculture: Is It Economic?" *Science*, June 6, 1969.

Cole, D. G. "The Myth of Fertility Dooms Development Plans." *National Observer*, April 22, 1968.

"Computers in Your Life—What They Can Do for You." *International Harvester Farm*, Fall 1965.

Cox, Bruce. "Sea Desalination." *Science and Technology*, April 1969.

Darlington, C. D. "The Origins of Agriculture." *Natural History*, May 1970.

Davenport, S., Jr. "Comeback of the Oyster." *New York Times Magazine*, December 20, 1970.

Delwicke, C. C. "The Nitrogen Cycle." *Scientific American*, September 1970.

Drew, E. B. "Going Hungry in America: Government's Failure." *The Atlantic*, December 1968.

Edwards, C. A. "Soil Pollutants and Soil Animals." *Scientific American*, April 1969.

"Farming in the Space Age." *International Harvester Farm*, Winter 1969–70.

Ghaswala, S. K. "Agricultural Research Blossoms: Fighting the Inefficiency that Brings Starvation." *Science News*, May 1968.

Gindertael, J. M. van. "Bigger Populations—Less Food." *UNESCO Courier*, March 1968.

Goro, Fritz. "New Challenges to World Hunger." *Life*, January 24, 1969.

Gray, W. D. "Fungal Protein for Food and Feeds." *Economic Botany*, January–March 1965.

———. "Fungi as a Potential Source of Edible Protein." *Activities Report*, Spring 1965 (Research and Development Associates).

"Growing Corn: the Shape of Things to Come." *International Harvester Farm*, Spring 1969.

Harpstead, D. D. "High-Lysine Corn." *Scientific American*, August 1971.

Harris, Marvin. "The Myth of the Sacred Cow." *Natural History*, March 1967.

"Helping Nature Control Insects." *Science News*, September 5, 1970.

"High Protein Hybrids." *The Sciences*, June 1969.

Hodge, C. O. "The Blooming Desert." *Bulletin of the Atomic Scientists*, November 1969.

Holt, S. J. "The Food Resources of the Ocean." *Scientific American*, September 1969.

International Flavors and Fragrances. "Rice . . . Food for Mankind." *The IFFer*, December 1968.

Isaacs, J. D. "The Nature of Oceanic Life." *Scientific American*, September 1969.

Jensen, M. H. "A Gift For the Desert: Power, Water, Food." *American Vegetable Grower*, November 1969.

Johnson, P. "Road, I Have Awaited Thee All My Life." *Ceres, the FAO Review*, September–October 1968.

Karasek, F. W. "Techniques for

211

Flavor Analysis." *Research/Development*, October 1969.

Kelly, C. F. "Mechanical Harvesting." *Scientific American*, August 1967.

King, K. W. "The World Food Crisis—A Partial Answer." *Research/Development*, September 1969.

Knoop, J. G. "Seeds on a Spindle." *The Farm Quarterly*, Fall 1968.

Lamm, M. "Fantastic New Farm Machines." *Popular Mechanics*, January 1970.

Levin, J. H. "Mechanical Harvesting of Food." *Science*, November 21, 1969.

"Little Fish, Big Fish." *The Sciences*, May 1969.

Mackey, A. C. "Cereals, Staff of Life, Take on New Importance in Today's World." *1969 Yearbook of Agriculture*, pp. 205–12.

McPherson, A. T. "Synthetic Food for Tomorrow's Billions." *Bulletin of the Atomic Scientists*, September 1965.

"Mechanical Mothers: Will They Replace the Sow?" *International Harvester Farm*, Summer 1968.

Meier, R. L. "The Social Impact of a Nuplex." *Bulletin of the Atomic Scientists*, March 1969.

Milner, M., ed. "Protein-Rich Cereal Foods for World Needs." The American Association of Cereal Chemists (St. Paul, Minnesota), 1969.

"New Guinea Natives: More on Nitrogen Fixing." *Science News*, August 29, 1970.

Oyster, H. E. "Meat and Vegetables Grown in Skyscrapers." *Edison Electric Institute Bulletin*, October 1967.

Patton, S., *et al.* "Food Value of Red Tide (*Gonyaulex polyedra*)." *Science*, November 10, 1967.

Pinchot, G. B. "Marine Farming." *Scientific American*, December 1970.

Pirie, N. W. "Leaf Protein as a Human Food." *Science*, June 24, 1966.

Platt, J. "What We Must Do." *Science*, November 28, 1969.

"Proteins from Pollutants—Making Dollars Out of Dross." *Chemical Engineering*, April 21, 1969.

Reinert, J. "Beefsteak from Bean Webs." *Science Digest*, September 1970.

Reitz, L. P. "New Wheats and Social Progress." *Science*, September 4, 1970.

Revelle, Roger (interview). *International Science and Technology*. June 1967.

Rowan, C. T., and Mazie, D. "Hunger—It's Here Too." *Reader's Digest*, November 1968.

Ryther, J. H. "Photosynthesis and Fish Production in the Sea." *Science*, October 3, 1969.

Scrimshaw, N. S. "The Potentials for Increasing World Protein Supplies." *Technology Review*, February 1970.

Sewell, W. R., et al. "Nawapa: A Continental Water System." *Bulletin of the Atomic Scientists*, September 1967.

Sigurbjörnsson, B. "Induced Mutations in Plants." *Scientific American*, January 1971.

Simpson, D. "The Dimensions of

Bibliography

World Poverty." *Scientific American,* November 1968.

"Soy Protein Debuts as Main Course." *Foods of Tomorrow,* Winter 1969.

Staub, W. J., and Blase, M. G. "Genetic Technology and Agricultural Development," *Science,* July 9, 1971.

Stewart, W. D. P. "Nitrogen-Fixing Plants." *Science,* December 15, 1967.

Streeter, C. P. "The Wheat Breeder Who Won the Peace Prize." *Farm Journal,* December 1970.

Tannenbaum, S. R., and Mateles, R. I. "Single Cell Protein." *Science Journal,* May 1968.

Tatum, L. A. "The Southern Corn Leaf Blight Epidemic." *Science,* March 19, 1971.

"This Hungry World." *The Rotarian* (Special Issue), June 1969.

Ugent, D. "The Potato." *Science,* December 11, 1970.

Uribe, Irene. "Behind the Rice Revolution." *Rockefeller Foundation Quarterly,* Fourth Quarter, 1968.

Vicente-Chandler, J. "Agricultural Potential of Latin America's Hot Humid Tropics." *Journal of Soil and Water Conservation,* March–April 1968.

Webb, B. H. "New Dairy Foods." *Food Engineering,* August 1970.

Wharton, C. R., Jr. "The Green Revolution: Cornucopia or Pandora's Box?" *Foreign Affairs,* April 1969.

Williams, C. M. "Third-Generation Pesticides." *Scientific American,* July 1967.

Woodwell, G. M. "The Energy Cycle of the Biosphere." *Scientific American,* September 1970.

Index

Picture Credits

Ford U.S. Tractor and Implement Operations, *13;* General Mills, *15;* Redrawn from Population Reference Bureau, *People!,* R. C. Cook and J. Lecht, eds., New York, Columbia Books, 1968, *18;* James Bouner, "The Next Ninety Years," in *The Next Ninety Years,* Pasadena, California Institute of Technology, 1967, *24;* A. H. Boerma, *Scientific American,* August 1970, p. 58, *27;* Paul R. and Anne H. Ehrlich, *Population, Resources, Environment,* San Francisco, W. H. Freeman and Company, 1970, p. 70, *37;* Adapted from *Research for the World Food Crisis,* D. G. Aldrich, Jr., ed., New York, American Association for the Advancement of Science, 1970, p. 200, *42;* S. H. Wittwer, in *Research for the World Food Crisis, op. cit., 49;* Rockefeller Foundation, *53;* Rockefeller Foundation, *55; Protecting Our Food: 1966 Yearbook of Agriculture,* Washington, U.S. Government Printing Office, 1966, *56;* U.S. Forest Service, *58;* Data supplied by International Minerals and Chemicals Corporation, *61;* Ford U.S. Tractor and Implement Operations, *62;* University of Minnesota, *65;* U.S. Department of Agriculture, *Contours of Change,* Washington, 1970, p. 32, *67;* S. H. Wittwer, "Research and Technology on the United States Food Supply," in *Research for the World Food Crisis, op. cit.,* p. 81, *66;* Pennsylvania State University, *69;* International Harvester Company, *72;* New York State College of Agriculture at Cornell University, *73;* Carle O. Hodge, University of Arizona, *75;* U.S. Department of Agriculture, *Foreign Agriculture Magazine,* December 22, 1969, *78* and *jacket.* International Harvester Company, *81;* U.S. Department of Agriculture, *82;* Rockefeller Foundation, *84;* Rockefeller Foundation, *85;* Rockefeller Foundation, *96;* Nigerian Consulate General, *97;* Edison Electric Institute, *103;* International Harvester Company, *105;* University of Arizona, *108;* Oak Ridge National Laboratory, *109;* Goodyear Tire and Rubber Company, *110;* Carle O. Hodge, University of Arizona, *112;* Edison Electric Institute, *114* and *115;* U.S. Department of Agriculture, *The Progressive Farmer, 115;* U.S. Department of Agriculture, *117;* USAEC, San Francisco Operations Office, *124;* Brookhaven National Laboratory, *125;* U.S. Department of Agriculture, *128;* General Foods, *129;* U.S. Department of Agriculture, *133;* International Flavors and Fragrances, *134;* General Mills, *141;* Texas Technological University, *144;* Clark Equipment Company, *147;* Esso Research and Engineering Company, *152;* The British Petroleum Company, Ltd., *154;* International Flavors and Fragrances/UNICEF, *156;* International Flavors and Fragrances, *158;* S. J. Holt, "The Food Resources of the Ocean," *Scientific American,* September 1969, *163;* Florida Power and Light Company, *170;* Florida Power and Light Company, *172; Scientific American,* December 1970, p. 21, *173;* International Minerals and Chemical Corporation, *180;* Louisiana State University, *183;* Pennsylvania State University, *185;* General Electric Research and Development Center, *186;* Battelle Memorial Institute, *189;* Pennsylvania State University, *190;* Cooperative for American Relief Everywhere, *200.*